Civic Engagement, Civic Development, and Higher Education

Civic Engagement, Civic Development, and Higher Education

Edited by Jill N. Reich
Bringing Theory to Practice
Washington, DC

1818 R Street NW, Washington, DC 20009

ISBN 978-0-9853088-3-4

Civic Engagement, Civic Development, and Higher Education

New Perspectives on Transformational Learning

EDITOR: Jill N. Reich

CIVIC SERIES EDITOR: Barry Checkoway

CONTENTS

FOREWORD

How can colleges and universities build capacity for civic engagement and civic development?

Previous monographs in the Civic Series have examined various ways of achieving this purpose—strengthening student learning, involving the faculty, and establishing campus-community partnerships. *Civic Engagement, Civic Development, and Higher Education,* the fourth in the series, focuses on the instrumental role of leadership and highlights the importance of individuals who are integral to the building process. Included among the authors are presidents, chancellors, deans, and distinguished professors who recognize the infrastructure required for implementation, and whose leadership takes the work to the next level.

These are individuals who have stepped forward with ideas, fueled by values and visions, that provide direction and inspiration for the work, without which little change is likely to last. These kinds of individuals are not the only ones involved in the building process, as change can originate almost anywhere in an institution, but they are among the most important.

The authors each operate in distinct types of institutions—including small and large, public and private, from community colleges to research universities—but, together, they recognize that individuals with ideas and inspiration are forces that help build capacity for the civic mission of higher education.

Barry Checkoway
General Series Editor

ACKNOWLEDGMENTS

This undertaking has had many sources and supporters over the years, from the first glimmer of the idea to this penultimate monograph in the Civic Series. Essential to its happening throughout its many forms is Donald W. Harward, director and cofounder of the Bringing Theory to Practice (BTtoP) project and former president of Bates College, whom I am honored to have worked with as a leader, a mentor, a person who inspires, and a friend. Both he and Sally Pingree, cofounder and supporter of the project, have nurtured an idea, a hope, into a force in higher education today.

Such forces do not happen, though, without many on the ground to translate ideas into reality, ensuring that what is necessary actually happens. Series editor Barry Checkoway works in quiet and mysterious ways, thoughtfully nudging ideas in more productive directions and being in the right place to teach important lessons, big and small. Dylan Joyce, BTtoP project associate, does more than assist. He has taken personal care to make certain that each author's ideas are carefully sustained throughout the editing process even as he works to ensure that each monograph proceeds on time and in situ. That he does so efficiently, effectively, and with patience is remarkable and much appreciated. I want to acknowledge the careful and detailed work of David Tritelli and Liz Clark, who assisted with the editing

and design of this volume. Finally, as we seek to build a model of higher education that is thoughtful, intense, intentional, and powerful, each member of the BTtoP team provides an example of how to accomplish this goal. For the insights and care of Ashley Finley, BTtoP national evaluator, and Jennifer O'Brien, BTtoP project manager, I am very grateful. You teach me in so many ways the true meaning of responsibility to others that is the foundation of transformative learning and flourishing.

Thank you to the authors of this volume who work so diligently and creatively on their own campuses but so willingly bring to us their best ideas and programs for stronger, more effective, and powerful learning opportunities on our campuses.

And to Richard, thank you for everything.

Jill N. Reich
Editor

ABOUT THE EDITOR

Jill N. Reich is professor of psychology at Bates College and senior scholar of the Bringing Theory to Practice project. From 1999 to 2011, she served as academic vice president and dean of faculty at Bates College.

INTRODUCTION
Jill N. Reich

HISTORICALLY, American colleges and universities have long recognized their responsibility to the public good. Often, to advance the public good was the reason for their founding, their purpose for educating, and a regular staple of their mission statements. But, while recognition of a civic role has been an integral part of American higher education, the understanding of this role and how to implement it changes as perceptions of and expectations for higher education develop to meet the demands of today and tomorrow. More recently over the past few decades, rather than seeing their civic role as implemented through service to the public, members and leaders of our colleges and universities are beginning to understand their civic role as one that is dynamic and reciprocal. In this context, bringing the civic into our institutions of high education must be accomplished in a way that is integral to the identity of higher education as a place for learning and creating new knowledge, a place for student development and well-being. This approach to the role of the civic in higher education "presupposes the importance of greater involvement by the public in the design and implementation of collaborative activities and also demands that faculty draw on their scholarly expertise for the benefit of the public as well as themselves."[1] It is an approach that understands college and university participation with the community as an intimate and necessary component of learning and knowledge creation for students, for faculty and staff, and for the community participants with whom they work.

Some leaders in colleges and universities wholeheartedly embrace this vision of their civic role, others are just beginning to see its value, and still others are focused on different parts of the academy—most often its intellectual component. The volumes in the Civic Series share the perspective that the very heart of higher education, its foundation and its passion, must emanate from the interactive and mutually reinforcing practice of transformative learning, civic engagement, and the flourishing or personal well-being that ensues from such an approach.[2] No one factor in this triumvirate can be ignored or eliminated; each depends on the others, and consideration of a unified approach ensures the greatest strength and meaning for higher education in the twenty-first century.

Many in the academy give a quick nod to the civic, as they focus instead on the intellectual demands of their programs with perhaps some attention to the personal well-being of their students. This is ironic since it is the civic, the attention to contributions beyond oneself, that gives meaning, power, and organization to intellectual and personal growth in just the ways that many in higher education seek to achieve[3] and that the public increasingly demands.[4] The essays in this volume confirm how greater attention to the civic reinforces these fuller purposes.

Each author presents a distinct approach from his or her own institution—from community colleges to research universities both public and private in the United States and the world beyond. Some consider initiatives that enhance educational excellence at the institutional level; others emphasize their work with faculty members, curricula, or communities; and still others explore the civic as expressed in the relationships of their institutions and communities, near and far. They include lessons learned from efforts to build a new institution from the ground up, to an institution working in cyberspace, to others working within systems with long-held traditions.

Some authors present how they intentionally bring the civic into their institutional spheres of work, while others describe how their efforts to build better and stronger learning communities have led them to the civic. No matter their distinct approaches, together they share a commitment to understanding what is, or can be, achieved by using the civic as an agent for change. They are involved in defining and redefining the civic for their institutions and building programs that are on the cutting edge of learning for tomorrow. In embracing the civic tradition of higher education, they are bearing witness to the fundamental beliefs that are the source of intellectual strength, personal well-being, and justice.

Great inspiration, much hopefulness, and good ideas will be found in their work.

NOTES

1. Crystal G. Lunsford, Burton A. Bargerstock, and Philip A. Greasley, "Measuring Institutional Engagement and Faculty-Based Engaged Scholarship," in *Engaged Scholarship, Vol 2: Community-Campus Partnerships*, ed. Hiram E. Fitzgerald, Cathy Burack, and Sarena D. Seifer (East Lansing, MI: Michigan State University Press, 2010), 105.

2. See Donald W. Harward, ed., *Transforming Undergraduate Education: Theory that Compels and Practices that Succeed* (Lanham, MD: Rowman & Littlefield, 2012) and other publications of Bringing Theory to Practice at http://www.BTtoP.org.

3. See Andrew DelBanco, *College: What It Was, Is, and Should Be* (Princeton, NJ: Princeton University Press, 2012); and George D. Kuh, *High-Impact Educational Practices: What They Are, Who Has Access to Them, and Why They Matter* (Washington, DC: Association of American Colleges and Universities, 2008).

4. See Richard Arum and Josipa Roksa, *Academically Adrift: Limited Learning on College Campuses* (Chicago: University of Chicago Press, 2011); and Ann Larson, "Higher Education's Big Lie," *Inside Higher Ed*, June 3, 2010, http://www.insidehighered.com/views/2010/06/03/larson.

PART 1 | Twenty-First-
Century
Institutions
and the Role
of the Civic

Civic Renewal of Higher Education through Renewed Commitment to the Public Good

1

Nancy Cantor and Peter Englot

WHAT WOULD A RESEARCH UNIVERSITY BE LIKE if we were to take seriously the admonition of the Kellogg Commission to reinvent ourselves for "the times that are emerging instead of the times that have passed"?[1]

Any answer to this question must be framed in the context of today's heightened scrutiny of higher education's value proposition. We operate, after all, in an era in which the returns on investment, the *private gains* of postsecondary education, are skyrocketing and yet the promise of the American dream—that education is a rightful pathway to social mobility—has hit a wall. There are shattered dreams and dim prospects for wide swaths of our population—indeed, especially for the fastest-growing, first-generation, minority (soon to be majority), and poor, which are frequently clustered in underresourced, underachieving urban and rural schools. The promise and the reality of higher education are two very different things for far too many students with potential in this country today, and we cannot afford to turn our backs on this talent pool of the future. Questions of access, diversity, and full participation must frame our civic renewal of higher education.

To address these urgent questions adequately, we must put our best efforts outside the academy first, starting with the schools and communities that are failing so many of our best and brightest from an early age. We can't sit back and wait for the exceptional few somehow to break through the barriers—economic, social, environmental, and cultural—that derail not only their individual educational progress, but also the progress of their communities writ large. We can't take a detached attitude toward the divisive and divided social and civic landscape of our times, where groups are pitted against each other and argue over individual rights rather than work to increase the seats at the table of educational opportunity for more of our talented students. We need to concentrate on the *public good,* knowing that any progress we can make in revitalizing our communities will down the line redound to the *private benefit* of more children, ensuring that we can educate the next diverse generation of civic leaders, professionals, and citizens, and reconnect more people to the American dream. In this sense, then, our efforts at a civic renewal of higher education—moving beyond our boundaries to engage in educational and scholarly partnerships in and with our communities—will drive the solutions needed to reinstate healthy pathways of access and opportunity.

CHANGING OUR WAYS

Any reinvention, therefore, must start from the premise that what we are doing now isn't sufficient to reignite the promise of the American dream of educational opportunity and its correlate of social mobility, at least not in a time of changing demographics, metropolitan challenges, and increasing disparities. Therefore, if we are to reinvent, we need to consider how higher education can become more publicly valuable—not just in technology transfer or in global reach, but in the places and with the people sharing those challenges of our times. Higher education needs to value its public mission—and acknowledge its social responsibility—before it can be truly valuable going forward.

Keeping in mind the failure of the American educational dream to be fully materialized in our time, we recommend four broad conceptual changes to guide the reinvention of the research university for the times that are to come.

1. From ivory towers to engaged institutions. The penchant to retreat from the world, even if in the service of constructing neutral communities characterized by unfettered debate and protected by academic freedom, is outdated. The conception of a "peaceful and thoughtful academy"—one standing apart from the fractured, hyper-partisan, and frequently brutal world in which we all live—not only isn't a true picture of many academicians' experiences, but also is at best a luxury and at worst somewhat irresponsible. It is true, physically and historically, that our campuses—many of which are located on hills overlooking our communities, as Syracuse University is—have for centuries been a place apart. Some of our buildings do resemble ivory towers, and we do have some gates and guards.[2] Down the hill are all the challenges of our rapidly urbanizing world—a degraded landscape, failing schools, pervasive poverty. All around us, we feel the tremors of the seemingly endless culture wars. As some contestants strive for a path to opportunity, others assume they can keep long-held privileges, and still others struggle for dear life to hold on to recently won gains.

But it is not true that the university is, can, or should be neutral territory, standing apart from the world. It is, in fact, an extremely contested piece of ground every single day. Certainly, members of marginalized groups and those identified as members of minority groups are keenly aware of this. It is hard to feel as if you fully belong when the threat of stereotyping follows you from the world outside the academy to interactions within it. The university is just as fraught with challenges—and ripe with possibilities—as is the world in which it is inextricably embedded. Instead of a zone of neutrality, which one might imagine as homogeneous and placid with "balanced," polite debates, the university more often resembles a battle zone where interest groups and disciplines and fervent disciples clash in fits and spurts, trying to gain ground or even survive to see another battle. By contrast, the university could instead be, or at least could aspire to be, a zone of diversity—inclusive not exclusive, engaging and energized by diverse perspectives and positions without needing a winning view, and engaged in dialogue across difference that recognizes our shared fates and responsibilities, both within the academy and in the wider world. We can get out of the ivory tower and fulfill our role as members of anchor institutions in our own communities, drawing connections to national and global contexts, but we need to relinquish some control and to operate in a much messier world than we are accustomed to in the academy.

That is precisely what we had in mind at Syracuse University when we began collaborating with a wide range of partners—public, private, nonprofit, academic—to develop the Connective Corridor, an urban pathway that traverses the city from the eponymous hill on which the university sits, across downtown, terminating in one of the region's oldest neighborhoods. This pedestrian- and bike-friendly route unites cultural venues, parks, public memory projects, and technology hot spots. A two-way "street" that is both physical and metaphorical, the Connective Corridor spurs conversations that flow both ways between the university and its many collaborators and generates one-of-a-kind engagement opportunities, including one of the largest urban video projects in the nation and an "Iconic Syracuse" billboard project developed by students in collaboration with the local historical association. That give and take is not only method-ologically optimal for our scholarship because it brings more perspectives to defining, analyzing, and solving problems, but it also immerses our students in the broader world where they can see how knowing and doing intertwine.

2. From meritocracies to cultivators of talent. Higher education effectively has ceded responsibility to define academic quality and college readiness to the popular press, whose measures tend to focus on inputs—such as the test scores of students before they enroll in college and on how many applicants colleges reject—and whose motives are primarily to sell more magazines or generate more click-throughs. Bill Gates captured the nonsensical—indeed, perverse—nature of such measures:

> If you try and compare two universities, you'll find out a lot more about the inputs—this university has high SAT scores compared to this one. And it's sort of the opposite of what you'd think. You'd think people would say, "We take people with low SATs and make them really good lawyers." Instead they say, "We take people with very high SATs and we don't really know what we create, but at least they're smart when they show up here so maybe they still are when we're done with them."[3]

What if, instead, we measured students' potential for success based on a wider portfolio, tapping entrepreneurial and leadership attitudes, taking into account where they have been and assessing where they might go—as, for example, the Posse Foundation does in its recruitment process?[4] In this context, we might credit universities as much for whom they reach as for whom they reject, and as often for how far their students go as for where they began. There are plenty of reasons to do just this.

Demographic shifts well underway are widening the already existing gaps in access to college. Fewer than 30 percent of students in the bottom quartile of family incomes manage to enroll in a four-year school. Of these, fewer than half graduate.[5] Even after accounting for financial aid, costs have gone up nearly 37 percent in the last twenty years at private institutions and 59 percent at publics (from a much lower base, of course),[6] while many students whose families need them to help out financially at home can't face years of lost wages and huge debts.[7] The already bad prognosis for income inequality and social mobility is worsened by the fact that often high-achieving, low-income students do not even apply to selective colleges, choosing instead to attend colleges that tend to have fewer resources and lower graduation rates.[8] We need to target our efforts at building the student bodies of our institutions in ways that will reverse these trends.

We can start in the communities of which we are a part. For example, at Syracuse University we partnered with the Say Yes to Education Foundation and the Syracuse City School District (SCSD), as well as the Syracuse Teachers Association, the county and city, and numerous other educational and community-based organizations in 2008 to work on closing the opportunity gap for an entire city's public schools by providing crucial, comprehensive socio-emotional, academic, health, financial, and legal supports for all twenty-one thousand city public schoolchildren and their families.[9] Through the Say Yes Higher Education Compact, SCSD students receive tuition support at fifty-four private institutions and New York State's public campuses. As of fall 2012, the compact had already supported more than 2,100 students in making the transition to college, including 174 to Syracuse University.

This approach to cultivating talent within communities also engages four-year institutions with community colleges in order to build hybrid models of educational opportunity such as are recommended in the Century Foundation's recent report *Bridging the Higher Education Divide*.[10] Moreover, by taking seriously our responsibility to cultivate talent broadly, we all become more attuned to the robust pool of talent in what we call "geographies of opportunity" in metropolitan regions around our nation—a talent pool we cannot afford to leave behind.

3. *From disciplinary silos to collaborative public scholarship.* Disciplines naturally branched out as the modern research university developed from the late nineteenth century; disciplinary norms and rewards developed and concretized right along with them, building a landscape of academic silos that persists today. Checklists for tenure and promotion decisions tend to reflect the same narrow forms of scholarship and restricted sets of publishing venues that they have for decades. Ironically, practically everyone in higher education today recognizes that these structures are ill suited to grappling with the messy, integrated, and critical problems we face on a global scale. Major funding organizations across the sciences, humanities, and arts have developed programs aimed specifically at breaking down these silos.[11] We within the academy must change our cultural norms to accelerate inter-, multi-, and trans-disciplinary collaboration.

Still, our traditions of defining what "counts" as scholarship can militate against embracing scholarly activities that look different from the prevailing disciplinary norms. We struggle to develop metrics attuned to the modes and methods of collaborative research and scholarship that cross sectors, involve funding that does not exclusively or even primarily accrue to the bottom line of the institution, and produce "products" that are difficult to count or attribute individually and whose impact may take considerable time to be realized.[12] Indeed, such publicly engaged scholarship can be a nightmare when viewed from the perspective of traditional counts—research dollars flowing through the university's budget, scholarly citations, short-term impact—yet it contributes powerfully to fulfilling higher education's role as a public good and, therefore, should count.[13] In fact, as we consider the diverse faculty of the future—many of whom are likely to have deep ties to communities and commitments to community partnerships, including working with students on publicly engaged scholarship and teaching—we will increasingly find not only that this scholarship *should* count, but also that it *must* count. This realization will require deep reflection on how to reward excellence in public scholarship, teaching, and engagement.

Making this happen is hard work. At Syracuse, it took us several years of sometimes heated debate, both about how to build into our institutional values and reward structures an explicit recognition of interdisciplinary, collaborative, and publicly engaged scholarship and about how to describe such scholarship in our faculty manual. But the benefits of this hard work are exquisite, generating scholarship that really makes a difference and creating the most engaging learning environments imaginable for our students. Working in tandem with the Tenure Team Initiative of Imagining America (an initiative led by Tim Eatman and Julie Ellison), our faculty senate revised the rules on promotion and tenure to acknowledge public scholarship, which may be published or presented in nontraditional ways. In addition, the Imagining America Publicly Active Graduate Education collaborative seeks to inspire and orient the next generation of graduate students differently, with all that portends, and they're getting the message.[14] As one participant, graduate student Janeane Anderson, blogged resolutely, "Far too often, academicians engage community organizations with preconceived knowledge hierarchies that privilege scholarship borne within the university over that which springs from the community. Mindsets that consider community-based knowledge as an addendum to scholarly work rather than something that stands alone must be changed in order to effectively integrate community-based expertise within the academy. New generations of academicians must fully embrace their dual citizenship within the academy and the community that surrounds the institution."[15]

4. From the "cult of the expert" to "communities of experts." Among the most persistent norms crystalized by the research university's development is the prevailing attitude of academics toward the role of nonacademics in the innovation process. This is seen nowhere more clearly than in the way universities tend to engage with research problems in their local communities, an approach evidencing what Harry Boyte has written eloquently about as a "cult of the expert."[16] Way too often, our "outreach activity" consists of one-off, short-term projects that are primarily one-way in character, and when "solutions" do arise out of this work, they never seem to last. In a similar vein, we have all heard from prospective private-sector partners that our rigid formulations for ascribing intellectual property create significant disincentives to pool expertise on problems from engineering healthier buildings to assuring consumer security in cyberspace.

To break down these self-imposed barriers, we need to leverage the role of our universities as anchor institutions. We need to create a two-way street of engagement with diverse, cross-sectoral, reciprocal partnerships—inside and outside of the academy—with "experts" with and without standard academic pedigrees. A pivotal aspect of this work will be building a more robust armature for ascribing and rewarding intellectual property rights that will catalyze cross-sector collaboration on innovation.

This is precisely the aim of our work on Syracuse's Near Westside, a "majority minority" neighborhood that includes the nation's ninth poorest census tract and faces challenges found in many urban communities nationally and globally, including high rates of crime, environmental degradation, illiteracy, poor health, and joblessness. Seven years ago, a group of residents joined with Syracuse University and with foundations, businesses, nonprofits, and officials in state and city government to create a new nonprofit organization, the Near Westside Initiative, dedicated to reasserting the strength of the community and tapping its often hidden potential. Instead of setting up a "command and control" model directed exclusively by university experts, the initiative adopted a collaborative model, asking participants to meet for consultation and discussion and to move toward a common goal. Although this process can be loud and messy, the result has been an environment that allows, inspires, creates, and sustains a host of innovative and successful collaborations of "experts" of all descriptions.[17]

SCHOLARSHIP IN ACTION

Enacting this multifaceted vision at Syracuse University has entailed recognizing that an innovative society and an inclusive society go hand in hand. We cannot solve the world's grand challenges without full participation by our entire talent pool—those with and without standard pedigrees, and those who do and do not fall squarely within our usual measures of high achievers. The way forward is to embrace an agenda that commits us to linking public problem solving with full participation, building a vibrant "architecture of inclusion," as Susan Sturm calls it,[18] on and off and between campus and community.

An innovative society and an inclusive society go hand in hand

A foundational aspect of this architecture is finding or forging the physical or metaphorical spaces where we can meet our partners from outside the academy in thought and action— "third spaces" that are not "owned" by any one partner and that constitute common ground where each participant's expertise is acknowledged and valued. The result is what the Association of American Colleges and Universities Caryn McTighe Musil sees as a new paradigm for "generative partnerships": traditional university-community boundaries are reimagined, partners employ democratic processes to achieve genuinely reciprocal engagement, institutions emphasize their citizenship, and effectiveness is measured by impact.[19]

These deep engagements intertwine education, public scholarship, and innovation even as they simultaneously open up our universities, bringing diversity, dialogue across difference, and "just academic spaces"—as Syracuse's Democratizing Knowledge faculty working group labels them[20]—back to campus. They lead us to transform how we do admissions, create inter-group dialogue curricula,[21] pursue and reward public scholarship, and view our institutional citizenship—

locally, nationally, and globally. In the process, faculty members in each discipline gain extraordinary opportunities to do work that is consequential both on the ground and in their fields, from envisioning and building urban landscapes that catalyze interaction among city residents to designing and implementing public health interventions in an innovative setting such as a community grocery store—all while exchanging and integrating ideas with professionals and with the toughest critics of all, end users in the community. At the same time, our public scholars are creating exceptional learning environments where their students can test their knowledge among this diverse and exacting "community of experts."

THE PATH FORWARD: UNIVERSITIES AS ZONES OF DIVERSITY, DIALOGUE WITH CONTEST, AND ENGAGEMENT

This kind of reinvention of the role and practices of the research university is aimed at fulfilling its public mission—its fundamentally democratic mission—by making a difference on the most pressing challenges of our day and simultaneously making progress on achieving the American dream of social mobility through education by training the next diverse generation of civically minded professionals, citizens, and leaders. Yet it is not for the faint of heart, as it involves working across traditional boundaries, enduring contested politics and heated dialogue, enacting a somewhat different version of academic freedom (a luxury perhaps more fitting when everyone is more or less alike on campus), and even bucking mainstream renditions of meritocracy (at least as enshrined in *US News & World Report* or in assessments of research powerhouses defined by institutional bottom lines). Reinventing the research university in this way is hard work, in part because it grounds noble intentions such as equity, fairness, inclusiveness, and shared responsibility that have long been embraced by higher education in the realities of specific places—our communities. It also relies on specific strategies for tapping the untapped talent within these places—suggesting, perhaps, the image of a nationwide "farm system" in which talented individuals in specific communities are cultivated, yielding a talent pool that serves the collective interests of all institutions and the public at large. (This agrarian metaphor aptly echoes the Morrill Acts in which higher education's public mission is ensconced).

As hard as this place-based work may be, the stakes are simply too high for us not to act decisively in order to shift higher education paradigms the way they need to be shifted. Not only the prosperity of individuals, but the prosperity of our democracy itself, hangs in the balance. As John Dewey once observed, "we have taken democracy for granted . . . it has to be enacted anew in every generation, in every year and day, in the living relations of person to person in all social forms and institutions."[22] In this light, it's always time for renewal in higher education, and today that means thinking and acting in ways that more clearly and demonstrably serve the public good.

NOTES

1. Kellogg Commission on the Future of State and Land-Grant Universities, *Renewing the Covenant: Learning, Discovery, and Engagement in a New Age and Different World*

(Washington, DC: National Association of State Universities and Land-Grant Colleges, 2000), 9.

2. Since this chapter was composed, the authors both have moved to Rutgers University-Newark. Illustrations of their work here are drawn from their time at Syracuse from 2004 to 2013.

3. Quoted in Jeffrey R. Young, "A Conversation with Bill Gates about the Future of Higher Education," *Chronicle of Higher Education,* June 25, 2012, http://chronicle.com/article/A-Conversation-With-Bill-Gates/132591.

4. The Posse Foundation conducts one of the nation's most innovative college access and youth leadership development programs in the nation, built around an understanding that prevailing definitions of academic talent and ability are too narrow. For a full description of its methodology for identifying talented students who might otherwise go unnoticed and cultivating them in partnership with colleges and universities, see http://www.possefoundation.org/about-posse.

5. Jason DeParle, "For Poor, Leap to College Often Ends in a Hard Fall," *New York Times,* December 22, 2012, A30–31.

6. Sandy Baum and Jennifer Ma, *Trends in College Pricing 2012* (New York: The College Board, 2012), 19–21.

7. DeParle, "Leap," A30.

8. Caroline Hoxby and Christopher Avery, "The Missing 'One-Offs': The Hidden Supply of High-Achieving, Low-Income Students," *Brookings Papers on Economic Activity* (Spring 2013): 1–65.

9. For a complete description of Say Yes to Education Syracuse, see http://www.sayyessyracuse.org.

10. The Century Foundation Task Force on Preventing Community Colleges from Becoming Separate and Unequal, *Bridging the Higher Education Divide: Strengthening Community Colleges and Restoring the American Dream* (Washington, DC: The Century Foundation, 2013).

11. To name but a few: the National Science Foundation describes as a "high priority" the effort to foster interdisciplinary research through programs such as Science, Engineering, and Education for Sustainability; Networking and Information Technology Research and Development and the National Nanotechnology Initiative (see http://www.nsf.gov/od/oia/additional_resources/interdisciplinary_research); the Mellon Foundation has been expanding its Research Universities and Scholarship in the Humanities program specifically to foster interdisciplinary work (see http://www.mellon.org/grant_programs/programs/higher-education-and-scholarship/researchuniversities); and the National Endowment for the Arts has convened the Federal Interagency Task Force on the Arts and Human Development in order to encourage more and better research on how the arts can help people reach their full potential at all stages of life—and task force members span the federal government, including the US Department of Health and Human Services, the National Institutes of Health, the National Science Foundation, and the US Department of Education (see http://nea.gov/national/TaskForce/index.html).

12. Questions about the time scale or schedule of "counting" are also critical. The traditional media-driven rankings are geared to selling magazines, year in and year out, and so they undervalue impacts and outcomes that take a while to evolve. They also tend to include slight variations on standard metrics in order to (somewhat artificially) introduce change in the rankings without really capturing the dynamics of what an institution is "doing" over time.

13. See, for example, the first-person accounts of publicly engaged scholars in Julie Ellison and Timothy K. Eatman, *Scholarship in Public: Knowledge Creation and Tenure Policy in the Engaged University* (Syracuse, NY: Imagining America, 2008).

14. Imagining America: Artists and Scholars in Public Life is a national consortium of publicly engaged artists, designers, scholars, and other community members working with institutions of higher education to enrich civic life. Drawing upon the humanities, arts, and design, the organization seeks to catalyze change in campus practices, structures, and policies that enables publicly engaged artists and scholars to thrive and contribute to community action and revitalization. Through its tenure initiative, Imagining America strives to facilitate discussion nationally about reforming tenure and promotion policies to account for publicly engaged scholarship. Another initiative, the Publicly Active Graduate Education program, cultivates graduate students to be publicly engaged scholars. Further information about Imagining America may be found at http://www.imaginingamerica.org.

15. Janeane Anderson, "Linked Fates: Why Campus-Community Collaborations are Necessary for Community Development," *PAGE Blog Salon* (blog), September 14, 2012, http://www.imaginingamerica.org/blog/2012/09/14/linked-fates-why-campus-community-collaborations-are-necessary-for-civic-development.

16. Harry Boyte, *Civic Agency and the Cult of the Expert* (Dayton, OH: The Kettering Foundation, 2009).

17. For a more complete description of this work, see Nancy Cantor, Peter Englot, and Marilyn Higgins, "Making the Work of Anchor Institutions Stick: Building Coalitions and Collective Expertise," *Journal of Higher Education Outreach and Engagement* 17, no. 3 (June 2013): 7–16.

18. Susan P. Sturm, "The Architecture of Inclusion: Interdisciplinary Insights on Pursuing Institutional Citizenship," *Harvard Journal of Law & Gender* 29, no. 2 (2006): 248–334.

19. Caryn McTighe Musil, "Connective Corridors and Generative Partnerships: A New Paradigm," *Diversity & Democracy* 16, no. 1 (2013): 6.

20. The Democratizing Knowledge project at Syracuse University is composed of critical scholars from interdisciplinary programs and departments whose self-described focus is "confronting white privilege, hegemonic masculinity, heteronormativity, and colonial heritages." Further information about the group may be found at http://democratizingknowledge.org.

21. A multi-university project under the direction of the University of Michigan's Patricia Gurin and her colleagues has developed exemplary, rigorous curricula and research on facilitating dialogue across differences among students, especially, but also including faculty and staff in higher education institutions and in K-12 schools. See Patricia Y. Gurin, Biren A. Nagda, and Ximena Zúñiga, *Dialogue Across Difference: Practice, Theory, and Research on Intergroup Dialogue* (New York: Russell Sage Foundation, 2013).

22. John Dewey, "Education and Social Change," *Bulletin of the American Association of University Professors* 23, no. 6, (1937): 472–3.

The Habit of Civic Engagement

2

Thomas L. "Les" Purce

FOR THE PAST FOURTEEN YEARS, I have been president of the Evergreen State College, a public liberal arts college in Olympia, Washington. Before returning to higher education some years before that, I was director of a state department of health and human services and had previously been mayor of a major city in Idaho. From the combination of these different positions, I have gained a unique perspective on some of the stress points in the fabric of our democracy.

As mayor, I saw up close many of the challenges facing our society—crime, stressed educational systems, and the ebb and flow of economies and their relationships to the success of small businesses and to poverty in local communities. I dealt with the same social ills on a bigger scale as director of a state department health and human services.

The view from those seats taught me that everyone pays a cost for a fraying social fabric. And while in my previous public roles I focused on addressing those pressing social problems, in higher education I have seen what I believe is a realistic, sustainable counterforce: students who are both inclined and competent to contribute to solutions that will sustain our democracy. Higher education is usually seen as primarily an academic endeavor, but academics widely integrated with engagement in the civic life of the community produces citizens who have a powerful, positive impact on society's challenges.

That truth was forcefully driven home for me when my past as a public administrator and my current academic role came together in the form of a single graduate. In 2009, at Evergreen's graduation celebration, a student named Tracy Guise approached me to point out that he and I had crossed paths before. Thirty years ago, Tracy had been a young boy in Idaho enduring a home life of abuse and neglect, and I was the director of the Idaho Department of Health and Welfare. Tracy was removed from his abusive family and taken into the care of the state. From there, he was soon adopted by a family in Washington State, where he found love and security. Tracy was delighted to inform me that, because I was director of Idaho Health and Welfare, my signature is on his adoption papers, and that now, because I am president of Evergreen, my signature is also on his college diploma. Thirty years before, the safety net caught Tracy Guise. It lifted him from a world of drugs, violence, and neglect, and landed him on Evergreen's commencement stage with a bachelor's degree in hand. I had the rare honor to stand at the bookends of that journey.

Today, Tracy works at Catholic Community Services Family Preservation. He helped found Gargoyles: Protectors of Children, a nonprofit organization formed by and for victims of childhood abuse and neglect. This organization is devoted to making the world a safer place for kids. At some point in Tracy's violent childhood, a city service—the police—intervened in his life in the name of public safety. A state agency then stepped in and took over his care, eventually leading to his successful adoption and a far safer, happier life. But it was at the Evergreen State College that Tracy was steeped in the practice, honed the skills, and, most importantly, built the commitment to civic engagement that he now exercises in order to improve the lives of abused and neglected children. The Tracy I met at graduation was a man of accomplishment surrounded by a loving family. He is a proud father, a proud biker, a proud protector of children, and a well-rounded, civically engaged citizen.

At Evergreen, we want our students to graduate with both the determination and the skills to take part in the civic life of their communities and to be willing agents for the public good.

It is common for higher education institutions to place students in internships and work experiences that help them form an understanding of issues in the community. Perhaps an issue will catch fire for a particular student, and he or she will devote time and attention to it after graduation. Too often, however, what students learn in their community experiences is isolated from the central focus of their academics, and it is left behind when they move on with their lives.

We at Evergreen believe that students need more than just exposure to social problems. They need also to exercise their civic muscles in such a way that engagement becomes muscle memory—habit, if you will. It is imperative that public liberal arts institutions begin the work of instilling the habit of civic engagement in their students before the fabric of our democracy frays beyond repair.

BUILDING THE HABIT OF CIVIC ENGAGEMENT
So what is necessary to build in students the habit of civic engagement? Students must attain a deep understanding of civic issues connected to and integrated into their academic endeavor. They must develop the appropriate engagement skills, and they must have real-world experiences in civic engagement. The ideal outcome will be that they have both deep knowledge about how the world works and the confidence to put that knowledge into practice throughout their lives.

What Evergreen has to offer as a model is rooted in the conviction that to educate successful and contributing graduates, academics and civic engagement must be integrated throughout the educational process in the same way that we integrate various disciplines in our interdisciplinary programs of study. Civic engagement involves skills that can be taught, but at its best the knowledge and commitment it requires grow out of the student's involvement with their academic studies—and very often the reverse, as well.

But civic engagement integrated with academics is not just something that we try to provide for or instill in our students. We have found that a college that both integrates and models engagement in its own actions and relationships is essential if graduates are to see the connection between their education and their lives as citizens. The college, too, has a responsibility as an institution within a community and the world to contribute to solutions that will sustain and strengthen the fabric of our democracy.

BRINGING THEORY TO PRACTICE

One of Evergreen's guiding principles is the concept of "theory to practice." In that spirit, I offer here a few examples of how we put this concept into action. Evergreen has always integrated community-based work into our academic programs. Our Center for Community-Based Learning and Action gets students into food banks, shelters, and classrooms, where they do good work that meets the community's unmet needs. Other examples can be found wherever our communities are struggling to respond to stresses in our societal fabric—the effects of mass incarceration, the urgent challenge of climate change, the education gap between rich and poor, and many other issues that challenge our communities.

One example is our Sustainability in Prisons Project, which brings science and nature into prisons. The project focuses on research and conservation projects that are carried out through collaboration among scientists, inmates, prison staff, students, and other community partners. The project reduces the environmental and economic costs of prisons, while encouraging sustainable and compassionate practices. The project, which is developing into a national network, varies from site to site. In Washington State, from 2005 to 2012, prisons recycled 2,000 tons of waste, composted 1,800 tons of food and landscaping waste, reduced solid waste to landfills by 47 percent, and decreased potable water usage by 100 million gallons annually. Scientists, students, inmates, and prison staff successfully raised endangered frogs and turtles for release into wetlands and rare plants for habitat restoration. The project also raises honey bees and butterflies to bolster struggling populations of crop pollinators.

Many of those participating in the project—both inmates and students—report that the experience of bringing nature into prisons is a life-changing experience. For some inmates, participation provides valuable job training and preparation for further education after release.

Similarly, our Gateways Programs for Incarcerated Youth brings Evergreen into juvenile correctional facilities, where our students sit with college-level incarcerated participants, working with Evergreen faculty to mentor youth working on attaining a GED or high school diploma. This award-winning and grant-supported initiative has high levels of documented success, with some of the incarcerated youth successfully making the transition to college upon their release.

Our Student Medical Assistant Program is another example of the full integration of academics and civic engagement. In this innovative program, students work in the campus health center as part of a multidisciplinary team, learning critical skills and earning credit for certification as medical assistants. As part of their education, they also work in community health education and outreach. Nearly all of the more than 150 graduates of this program have gone on to become physicians, nurse practitioners, physician assistants, or alternative providers such as acupuncturists or naturopaths. Many have returned to their communities to practice.

Recognizing the importance of the early integration of academics and engagement in a student's experience, Evergreen recently created the first annual Evergreen Student Civic Engagement Institute (ESCEI). This week-long institute for incoming students is held just before our regular new student orientation. While all newly admitted students are invited, the institute has room for approximately fifty students who are selected on the basis of a relatively simple application. We have five primary goals for the institute:

1. We want students to learn how to engage productively with the community, both during their time on campus and in their personal lives well beyond their years at Evergreen.
2. We want to help students become leaders on campus and in their lives beyond campus.
3. We want students to discover how to deal with complex and often controversial topics in a civil and respectful manner.
4. We want to challenge students both intellectually and socially, to move them beyond their personal comfort zones, and to encourage them to begin to see the world through the eyes of others.
5. We want to engage students early and, thus, increase their retention relative to the rest of our undergraduate population.

The institute offers a robust curriculum that engages students in a variety of activities. In the first iteration in the fall of 2013, students took part in a day-long conflict resolution workshop run by staff from the Seattle-based William D. Ruckelshaus Center, whose mission is to serve "as a neutral resource for collaborative problem solving in the State of Washington and Pacific Northwest." They were also trained in ways to look for consensus when dealing with particularly controversial issues by staff from the Community Forums Network, another Seattle-based organization whose mission is to "bring people together to talk about important issues and to discover consensus."[1] Additionally, the students spent a day working at a local nonprofit organization, after listening to a panel of local community organization leaders discuss the work they do and how others can help. Finally, the students participated in a seminar on Dave Isay's wonderful book *Listening Is an Act of Love.*[2] The book focuses on the value of listening to others and demonstrates how careful and respectful listening can bring people together. Because each of the college's incoming students had received a copy of the book, students who participated in the institute were able to use some of their leadership skills in the week following the institute at orientation as they joined in broader discussions of the text with their new colleagues.

The academic component of the engagement institute continues through the fall quarter, when each student is expected to select an individual or group project designed to enhance the leadership and civic engagement skills developed during a concurrent ESCEI course. The projects have varied widely. Two past students volunteered at the local food bank and then presented information about the related program's efficacy to fellow students in a number of classes.

Another past student developed an advertising campaign for National Mental Health Awareness Day.

We have every expectation that some of the participating students will become student leaders, capable of providing meaningful direction to on-campus organizations and able to help improve the quality of discourse about some of the complex issues that invariably arise on our campus. Beyond that, we hope and expect that, after graduation, these students will become leaders in their local and wider communities and will remain engaged throughout their lives.

The National Center for Public Policy and Higher Education noted in 2008 that, in the new century, "the confluence of social, economic, and political forces pose daunting new challenges to the nation's vitality. . . . Higher education must organize its resources for increased responsiveness to and engagement with society's core challenges in the century ahead."[3] The intent of the original Morrill Act, the 1862 federal law that established land-grant universities, was not only to educate youth in the sciences and professions, but also explicitly to produce leaders and contributors to local communities. That expectation and motivation has never been more important.

One of the greatest threats facing higher education today is the growing belief that what college and universities do is only of private benefit to our graduates, and that we can be judged not only on whether our graduates are employed, but also on whether they are among the highest earners. If this belief that the sole purpose of higher education is to enable graduates to make as much money as they can is allowed to persist, then it will become easy to make the case that higher education is an entirely private good. This belief devalues the critical importance of preparing students to be effective citizens of our democracy, and it thoroughly undercuts the responsibility of the state to support our institutions.

These students will become leaders in their communities and remain engaged throughout their lives

At Evergreen, we continue to look for ways to expand the measure of our success as producers of graduates who see themselves as both breadwinners and community builders, as people with the skills, the confidence, and the habit of civic engagement. At Evergreen, we constantly look for opportunities to help students like Tracy Guise find ways to ignite and actualize their passions—passions that may well transform them and their communities.

NOTES

1. These descriptions and full information about the William D. Ruckelshaus Center and Community Forums Networks can be found on their websites, http://www.ruckelshauscenter.wsu.edu and http://www.communityforumsnetwork.org, respectively.

2. Dave Isay, ed., *Listening Is an Act of Love: A Celebration of American Life from the StoryCorps Project* (New York: Penguin, 2007).

3. Gregory R. Wegner, *Partnerships for Public Purposes: Engaging Higher Education in Societal Challenges of the 21st Century* (San Jose, CA: National Center for Public Policy and Higher Education, 2008).

Civic Learning in Community Colleges

3

Brian Murphy

IN THE FALL OF 2013, students at De Anza College succeeded in two campaigns they had begun a year before. First, they reached an entirely friendly accord with the college bookstore not to sell clothing produced with sweatshop labor. Second, they persuaded the Foothill-De Anza Community College Foundation to divest itself of investments in fossil fuel companies as part of a campaign aligned with a national 350.org campaign targeting top corporate polluters.[1]

In both instances, the student groups marshaled evidence, made powerful arguments based on that evidence, and demonstrated that they represented a significant swath of student opinion. They were careful and deliberate, creating alliances with faculty and staff, listening to counter arguments, and seeking more data when required. They stood for clear principles of social justice, equity, and environmental sustainability. As they mobilized, and amended their positions as needed, they taught us—their faculty and staff allies. They did not back off; they did not back down; they did not quit. And they won.

Their victory was ours as a campus community. As one of the Foothills-De Anza College Foundation board members told the students before the final, unanimous vote, "We learned from you. We would not have brought this up ourselves, or known what our options were. Thank you." There was a sense of solidarity and connection between the student organizers and the community leaders who volunteer their time for the foundation, a sense that they stood together and stood for something. And there was also appreciation on both sides: that the foundation would be so open to the divestment argument, and that the students would be so thoughtful in their campaign.

The divestment was the first by any community college foundation in the country, and symbolized a connection between community college organizers and their university counterparts that took everyone by surprise. The 350.org campaign on fossil fuel divestment had focused on major universities with enormous endowments, as well as on state universities. The anti-sweatshop movement is similarly well established in American universities, with a variety of protocols banning sweatshop goods. In neither instance were community colleges or their students envisioned as part of the movement, or as a source of leadership.

Yet activism is deeply embedded in the culture at De Anza College. Undocumented students and their allies were deeply involved in the fight for the DREAM Act,[2] students organized for the living wage in San José, and still others participated in annual budget fights in the state capitol. These movements and mobilizations reflect a much deeper cultural element of the college: a shared commitment to the idea of civic identity. Our students want, need, and demand an education into their social and civic environments, and the tools to change both.

In this orientation, De Anza stands against the dominant narrative in American higher education, and has sister community colleges across the country committed to the idea that our students deserve more than to be treated as if they have no civic life and do not need to understand how power works.

THE CIVIC NARRATIVE AT DE ANZA
De Anza College is one of California's top community colleges. The California Community College System includes 112 colleges,[3] all publicly funded. De Anza is a large and complex institution, with 23,000 students, dozens of degree and certificate programs, and a reputation for successful transfer to universities. The college understands itself as a regional institution serving the multiple communities of San José and Silicon Valley. Our student body is extraordinarily diverse, with no racial or ethnic "majority." Our students are 42 percent Asian (Chinese, Vietnamese, Filipino, Korean, and Indo-Americans), 23 percent Latino, 20 percent white, and 5 percent African American. Nine percent are international students.

Our students are diverse in all ways. The student body includes very well prepared recent high school graduates as well as those who have dropped out and never graduated, workers returning for retraining, and recent immigrants learning English. Thousands of our students view De Anza as the first and best step in a long educational passage. They are most often the first in their families to go to college. A key question we at De Anza Community College ask ourselves is this: what narrative do we build not for them, but with them, to frame what we do?

Let's start here. Eighty-five percent of our students do not test at college level in math or reading, so one approach could be to focus on their needs, or deficits. Our narrative would then be about opportunity and about offering each underprepared student the chance to overcome their deficits and become skilled and employable. But there is an alternative approach: to start with the manifest strengths of our students. We begin our narrative with this: 70 percent speak at least two languages, many have navigated the social and linguistic transitions of immigration, and both documented and undocumented students have managed their way through the public and private bureaucracies seemingly designed to make life difficult for them. They get up each morning, by the thousands, and get themselves to school. They have skills and capacities, in short, well beyond their test scores and their nominal "deficits."

Most critically, they are not alone in their passage. Most come from communities, families, and networks of extended relations that are interdependent and that require responsibility and agency. They come with rich social identities that frame their expectations and hopes and dreams.

De Anza sees its students through this alternative lens. They are talented and capable, able to act on their own behalf—especially when they act with each other. They come to a college without adequate state-funded resources or staff, but one that asks them to step up and help each other. They come to a commuter college, but one with vibrant student extracurricular programs and clubs, a student government with an independent budget of more than $1.5 million, and an athletic program that demands excellence in academics as well as athletics. The campus is alive with activity and energy; it's a place to hang out and talk and see your friends—despite the fact that most students work, many full time.

We start our story with the talents and capacity of our students. Then our narrative is framed by the grace and skill they bring to building a respectful campus environment in which diversity is genuinely appreciated. They come from a multicultural environment new in the United States, one in which they have to navigate their differences of perception and presumption in virtually every daily encounter, every class, and every social gathering. They are building a community among themselves that will be of great significance for their later lives in the new California and the changing United States.

Do they get it right all the time? No. Do they—and we—trip and make mistakes that force us all to confront contradictions we had never thought about before? You bet. Are there moments of tension and struggle and fear and rejection and doubt? Yes. But through it all there is a faculty and a staff deeply committed to the newly emerging community and to the idea that the college is about the development of a civic personality among our students, in addition to the mastery of their disciplines and their fields of study. Only when they have developed this wider range of skills will they be able to navigate the social complexities of their demography, the region's economy, and the nation's politics.

How does this actually work? We have created institutional structures explicitly devoted to the civic dimension of our community, and we integrate civic work into the curriculum. The college supports the autonomous agency of our students, whether it is exercised through student government, student clubs and organizations, student organizing, or the spontaneous occupation of public spaces for poetry, music, and hip-hop. The physical design of the campus emphasizes free and open public spaces for students to work, play, pause and reflect, organize. The college leadership—both administrative and faculty—is explicit about its conviction that our students will play a public and civic role in their communities and that the college seeks to engage them in this dimension of their lives.

A key example of this conviction is the De Anza College Institute for Community and Civic Engagement (ICCE), which is home to both curricular and extracurricular civic projects. ICCE sponsors a robust and ongoing conversation among faculty, staff, and students about how to engage more students in community-based work, political and social movements, and course projects that integrate current economic and social issues. In the fall of 2013, ICCE sponsored a Public Policy School that brought local leaders to campus in order to teach about advocacy and political change. The college offers a certificate in social change leadership, and it graduates students who have been formally trained as organizers. Our transcripts clearly note community service courses taken; we provide support and public recognition for student leadership.

The goal of developing the civic identity of our students is embedded in program design and curricula across the campus. Our increasing use of learning communities reflects the work of many faculty to design courses around students' capacity to responsibly help each other, work together, and make sure others learn. One example of such a learning community is LEAD (Latina/o Empowerment at De Anza), a program that enrolls more than 450 students each quarter in English, Sociology, and other courses where all students work in small groups called *familia*—each with a peer mentor, each with a community-based project, and in which each member of the *familia* takes responsibility to ensure that every other member fully engages in the work.[4] The success rate in these courses (passing with an A, B, or C) is 92 percent.

LEAD courses focus on topics related to the Latino experience; but enrollment is open, and Latinos account for only roughly half of all enrollees. The program has been so successful that it has been used as the model for IMPACT AAPI (Initiatives to Maximize Positive Academic Achievement and Cultural Thriving focusing on Asian American and Pacific Islander students at De Anza College), a similar five-year program for underserved Asian students funded by an AANAPISI (Asian American and Native American Pacific Islander-Serving Institutions) grant from the US Department of Education.[5] Both programs have developed cohort models that depend on the capacity of our students to work collaboratively, across differences of language, history and culture. The cohort model is also used in our auto tech program, which has long been known for its quality and now for new curricula in electric and hybrid design. Beyond technical certifications, the auto tech program prepares students for leadership in their communities. The students work as integrated teams, learning with and supporting each other, and asking how they can serve the broader community. They see their work itself as a civic act, helping people make the transition to alternative fuels. And each year, the Auto Tech Club is the single largest donor to the area food bank in a region that celebrates its innovation and wealth and does too little to help the one in four families who are hungry.

These are examples of a college devoted to an alternative view of its students, and to an alternative narrative about education. In this narrative, students come with robust social identities, however uneven their formal educational backgrounds may be. They seek transfer and certification and employable skills in a regional economy in which 40 percent of the jobs require a bachelor's degree. But they know that their families and their communities will need more than employment; the students will need to know how to work across the divisions of class, race, and language that fracture the region, and they will have to understand how public and private power works. An education that fails to prepare them for these questions is one designed to marginalize them. An education that includes civic learning gives students the tools to discover and develop their own agency and power.

THE NATIONAL CONTEXT: A MOVEMENT AND A CHALLENGE
De Anza College is not alone among America's community colleges in this view of students and their education. Indeed, we are now part of a national community

college movement explicitly devoted to the development of the democratic capacity of our students. The Democracy Commitment (TDC), founded only in 2010, now has more than 130 community college campuses in its national network, enrolling over 2,300,000 students. They range in size from small regional colleges like Allegany College of Maryland to large urban districts like Maricopa in Arizona and Miami Dade in Florida. There are TDC colleges across the country, in Texas, Ohio, Oregon, California, New York, and more than fifteen other states.

The Democracy Commitment is just that: a commitment by community colleges that their students will receive an education in the practical skills of democracy, and the civic knowledge with which citizens (and non-citizens) can navigate the institutions of public life. There is no one template for this work; it can range from community service learning to the civic activism of community organizing. It can be deeply rooted in degree and certificate programs that aim to transfer students to four-year universities or embedded in career and technical programs that aim to move students into the workforce. It can involve student clubs, extracurricular programs, and student government. It can mean partnerships between colleges and local nonprofit and community groups.

But whatever form it takes, a commitment to the democratic capacity of our students requires institutional intentionality and public conversation about this dimension of the work. It must be part of the college mission and strategic planning. It must be part of institutional life, embedded in faculty conversation and openly acknowledged as contested terrain, not settled doctrine. What does "civic agency" mean in career/technical programs? What is the civic dimension of a discipline? What are alternative views regarding the practical knowledge our graduates need to navigate ever-changing economic and political environments? In other words, we must have the conversations we want our students to have, and with the same openness to difference and debate.

A commitment to the democratic capacity of our students requires institutional intentionality and public conversation

The Democracy Commitment brings this work into a national conversation, and it provides a space where those committed to civic engagement can meet each other and reach out to their counterparts. For De Anza College, TDC offers support and affiliation as well as a place where our people can talk with others who reject the deficit model so prevalent in the national narrative about our students. And, finally, TDC connects community college work with the universities where so many of our students transfer. TDC lives in a partnership with the American Democracy Project, the now ten-year-old coalition of 242 universities sponsored by the American Association of State Colleges and Universities (AASCU). It is not lost on our colleagues at AASCU institutions that more than half of their graduates are transfers from community colleges. Our students are their students.

Our challenge is to expand our coalition of institutions further, to bring more community colleges and four-year colleges into partnerships that reinforce the value and power of civic work. De Anza College and other TDC members are working to ensure that any movement aiming to retrieve the "civic" from the margins must include the nation's community colleges and our students.

NOTES

1. The mission of the Foothill-De Anza Foundation is to change student lives by raising and investing funds to support the educational excellence of Foothill and De Anza Colleges. See http://www.foundation.fhda.edu. 350.org was founded in 2008 as a global climate movement to link climate-focused campaigns, projects, and actions by people from 188 countries who lead from the bottom up. See http://www.350.org.
2. The DREAM Act is a piece of bipartisan legislation designed to provide qualified undocumented immigrant youth eligibility for a six year long conditional path to citizenship. At the time of this publication, the DREAM Act legislation has not been passed into law. See http://www.dreamact.info.
3. For further details about the California Community College System, see http://www.cccco.edu.
4. For further details about LEAD, see http://www.deanze.edu/lead.
5. For further details about IMPACT AAPI, see http://www.deanza.edu/impact-aapi.

Making Civic Engagement Matter to More Students: Expanding Our Reach and Improving Our Practice

4

Paul LeBlanc

MANY PEOPLE FEAR that online education makes it harder to support civic education and engagement, worrying about isolated and alienated students (the antithesis of civic engagement, really) sitting behind computer screens at home and alone. It need not be so. In fact, a new generation of degree programs—online and competency based—can actually empower previously marginalized adult learners from around the globe with new knowledge and powerful tools to shape their worlds, while dramatically improving and expanding civic education and engagement. Because these programs largely serve adult learners—the majority of college students today—they also expand civic engagement's generally narrow focus on traditional-age students in residential "coming of age" settings. While these next-generation competency-based approaches are still new, they have remarkable potential to make civic education both better and more broadly available.

First, some background. Southern New Hampshire University made history in April 2013, when its College for America (CfA) degree program became the first competency-based program to be approved by the US Department of Education. While competency-based programs have been around for a long time, CfA is the first approved program fully to untether from the three-credit-hour construct, or Carnegie Unit. Working online and at their own pace, CfA students must demonstrate mastery of 120 competencies—there are no courses or classes—and they can go as fast or as slow as they like. The first CfA graduate went from zero credits to completing an associate's degree in only three months, because in CfA learning is fixed and time is variable. The key breakthrough with CfA is a fundamental reversing of the Carnegie Unit, which makes it very easy to report how long students have sat in classrooms, but not to measure what they actually learned while there.

Competency-based education, by its very nature, is very clear about the claims it makes for student learning, and it is complemented (or should be) by well-designed assessments that force students to demonstrate mastery. In contrast, traditional higher education tends to be much less precise about what graduates *actually know,* with the exception of fields where there is rigorous third-party certification (think nursing boards for nursing or the CPA exam for accountants). Indeed, much of traditional higher education actively resists such accountability.

Commensurately, at most institutions, civic engagement often feels squishy—ill-defined, poorly assessed, and touching only a percentage of the graduates. In a program like CfA, there is no room for the ambiguous or ephemeral. There are well-defined competencies related to civic learning, engagement, and responsibility, and students complete projects that concretely demonstrate their mastery against rubrics that reviewers use to assess the work.

IMPROVING OUR PRACTICE BY CLARIFYING OUR CLAIMS

CfA includes competencies necessary to participate fully as citizens in the broader society (e.g., critical thinking, communication skills, media literacy) and pays special attention to ethics and social responsibility in various key societal contexts (science/technology, media, business). More importantly, competency-based education does not have to be vocational or merely utilitarian, as some traditionalists fear; the work can require higher-level thinking and critical analysis, and it is well-suited for the kinds of learning widely associated with civic education. Moreover, by resting on a strong foundation of clear competencies and well-defined rubrics required for demonstration of mastery, competency-based education offers greater clarity about learning than do many traditional programs.

In an exploration of torture, for example, the competencies include the ability to describe major traditions in moral philosophy, to identify key figures in the field of moral philosophy and explain their views, and to identify and evaluate ethical arguments. Other competencies include the ability to research, write, and edit one's own work. Every student has to complete these competencies; there is no sliding by with a B or C (one has either "mastered" or "not yet"), and they are not "add-ons" to the educational experience. These competencies are built in and expected of everyone with the CfA associate's degree. In terms of rigor, accountability, and quality, competency-based education is transparent and coherent in ways that the mere "weaving in" of civic learning is not. Built into the program as it is with CfA, no students are left out.

To illustrate, one area of study for the associate's in general studies degree requires that students examine ethical perspectives. In this area, students explore a variety of essential ethical questions—whether torture is ever justified, for example, or whether people should be able to sell their own organs. In another area of study, students consider the environment by examining the environmental impacts of common products—like bottled drinking water—and show whether they can both calculate the specific carbon footprint of the industry and generate solutions to mitigate it. Students must show that they can identify and analyze ethical issues raised by scientific and technologic developments by analyzing the infamous Johns Hopkins Lead Paint Study (in which researchers put children in potentially dangerous living situations) and determining whether or not it violated ethical principles of science.[1] They engage in questions about globalization and the meaning of "corporate responsibility." They look at advertisements and examine the ethical issues involved—for example, in marketing to children. They also read important thinkers on the questions under consideration. For example, in the torture example, students read Michael Sandel's *Justice: What's the Right Thing to Do?* and Sam Harris's "In Defense of Torture,"[2] and they study Mill on utilitarianism and Kant on duty-based ethics. Their work is assessed against a well-defined rubric that asks them to spot issues, apply relevant philosophies, provide evidence for their analysis, and identify ethical flaws in the argument. In these examples, students engage very explicitly with the kinds of thinking, analysis, and application of ethics that support civic learning. In CfA, there is greater clarity of claims about and confidence in the actual learning (and the ability to demonstrate both) than most institutions possess. And because these elements of civic learning are explicitly built into the curriculum, they become crucial to it. Students cannot graduate without completing these competencies, and they are not the tangential add-ons one sees in many institutional efforts.

Not only can competency-based education offer a way to strengthen what counts as civic learning but, by leveraging its lack of geographic boundaries, it can also broaden definitions of community in ways that more traditional campus-based efforts tend not to do. As Dan Butin noted, the great majority of faculty members think about civic engagement in terms of local community.[3] But CfA's online programs collapse traditional assumptions about what community means. For CfA students, enrolling through their employer and interacting with colleagues in multiple sites, the "company" can become the community. By enlisting employer engagement in ways that colleges usually do not, CfA is altering the way students "live" within that community of work: they now forge relationships with fellow employees across the company (and its multiple sites), are newly empowered within the workplace, and have a higher level of recognition and, thus, responsibility with their employer.

CfA can push the boundaries of community much further in online programming. In a discussion of environmental issues, online students can be part of a global community addressing a global issue. In this case, civic learning becomes less a case of the privileged "helping the needy"—as so often is the case in service-learning programs, for example—and more a case of genuine engagement with "others" whose claim to a stance on the environment is no less privileged than that of students in the United States. Or in another example, stereotypical and clumsy claims about the veil in Islam might have a very different hearing when students in the class are logging in from Saudi Arabia and Qatar and Paris. The problems that need to be solved today—whether related to climate change, economic inequity, fundamentalism, or corporate irresponsibility—extend well beyond the more localized sense of community that most faculty members favor. In a globally connected world where coal burning in China affects air quality and asthma rates in Chino, California, and where a Koran burning in Florida results in rioting and deaths in Pakistan and Afghanistan, online platforms and tools allow for the global definition of community and, thus, civic engagement in ways that traditional classrooms can't touch.

Serving More Students and Expanding Our Impact

However, the starting point with CfA students is often not that of getting them to think beyond their local communities; it is, rather, to start with a recognition that they are part of a community *of any kind.* Discussions of civic engagement and learning almost always assume that students are eighteen-year-olds in traditional coming-of-age residential four-year colleges. But according to the National Center for Education Statistics, that student profile is a distinct minority today.[4] Online programs mostly serve older adults for whom education gets squeezed between the demands of family and work. For CfA students, the world has often found ways to exclude them from community through conditions of poverty, dysfunctional neighborhoods, alienated and disrespected labor, and more. Yet these students deserve and need the benefits of civic learning and engagement no less (perhaps much more) than their traditional-age peers.

I would go a step further. The need to *re-engage* civically might be even greater for the student most marginalized by traditional education and often by society at large, for one who has never felt a sense of "mattering," as Brown Sociologist Greg Elliott and his colleagues use the term: "A relatively new concept, 'mattering' is the belief persons make a difference in the world around them. Mattering is composed of three facets—awareness, importance, and reliance. Do others know you exist? Do they invest time and resources in you? Do they look to you as a resource? Elliott asserts that mattering is the fundamental motivation in human beings. 'Above all else, there's a need to matter,' he says."[5]

CfA students are often hourly workers in food processing plants, convenience stores, and manufacturing plants, and most are long removed from education at any level. Statistically, they are much less likely to be civically engaged than their college-educated peers (in our increasingly socioeconomically divided society, they probably don't have many college-educated *neighbors*), and they come to CfA with little perceived social capital and few tools to leverage it. So, to the extent that it addresses those needs, the *delivery* of the CfA program is proving almost as powerful as the competencies and topics included in the CfA degree.

CfA students engage with the CfA community, both online and in person, in a variety of ways in order to build their own learning and, eventually, professional networks. Students become members of a learning community while completing their competencies through peer interactions—asking and answering questions, providing feedback, sharing resources, and celebrating successes. However, in the CfA model, students are also asked to think about and leverage other resources in their lives. They are asked to name an "accountability partner," someone whom they can trust to keep them on pace and on task (the way a "gym buddy" increases the likelihood that one will get out of bed and to the gym to work out). They are asked to think about workplace mentors upon whom they can call for help. Some activities require students to work in teams, and all students get a Southern New Hampshire University coach who supports them throughout their degree program. Maybe the most powerful motivator is the way employers let CfA students know it matters to them that they are enrolled. While most employers simply sign off on tuition reimbursement, CfA employer partners are encouraged to let their employees know they care and are invested in their success.

The first step in becoming engaged in the community—in any community— is to think of oneself as first belonging and then as empowered—a sense that grows with CfA students, who form workplace "meet ups" on their own and find ways to support each other. CfA then builds on that sense of community with requirements that they start engaging in professional networks such as LinkedIn as part of a competency called "establishing a professional presence." In fact, social capital theory and social media tools are a critical part of CfA's design. The CfA portal allows students to see who else in their company is enrolled (in design studies, students identified this as very important to them), who else is working on the same competencies, and who else has successfully completed which competencies (since they might then become a peer-to-peer learning resource). CfA has no instructional faculty, so this peer-to-peer engagement serves learning needs while also building a sense of community. It does so not only from a sense of belonging and shared experience, but also through the empowering confidence that comes from helping peers.

As important as the interactions between students are the specific tools that enable them. For example, all CfA students are asked to join a Google Plus Community—a social networking site that allows students to connect with each other and other mentors in CfA. Using that powerful platform, students can do the kind of interactions described previously: ask questions about the projects they are working on, about technical issues, or about the program more generally. Information technology and academic experts monitor the community to answer questions, but more often than not, other students will respond before those experts get a chance. All the coaches are also active in the community, posting resources on success strategies and tools for completing academic work. The Google Plus community also allows students to connect with each other privately in order to collaborate on team projects or to discuss other issues that might be important to them. CfA employs a range of other Google tools to support academic work and community building as well. Students check in with their coaches, complete team projects, and submit presentations over Google Hangouts—a free video-conferencing service. They use Google Docs to critique each other's writing.

The first step in becoming engaged in any community is to think of oneself as belonging and then empowered

To some extent, it is taken for granted that traditional-aged students have some facility with such tools. But for the adult students CfA serves, these are tremendously empowering tools to master. Social media tools are now critical components of any community interaction at any level, from organizing fundraising walks to political campaigns to rebellions in the Arab World. Not to possess mastery of these tools is to be marginalized and often left out; digital literacy is becoming as important as reading and writing. CfA provides practice in the use of these tools, models their application, and demonstrates their power. The extent to which students answer questions before the staff do, or organize meet-ups offline, or go out to access resources and people outside of the CfA program and community provides assurance that they are being equipped with some elements of the essential toolkit of modern civic engagement in a society of technology haves and have-nots.

There is a core assumption in all that has been thus far outlined: that CfA graduates will take all they have learned, the tools they have mastered, that sense that they matter, and actually become more civically engaged after they graduate.

This is something that will be assessed and tracked over time, as the first CfA graduates have been—and as should also be done for the civic engagement programs in more traditional settings. In the meantime, if one were designing a new program for civic engagement at one's institution, the following would be a pretty good checklist of priorities:

- Be very clear about how civic engagement is defined, measured, and built into the curriculum.
- Include ethics education across fields and areas that shape community and civic life (such as media, corporate responsibility, the environment, and more).
- Expand the definition of community and make sure students engage with others who are quite different from themselves on some sort of equal footing.
- Give students the technological tools to engage in this way.
- Provide students with a sense that they matter and that they have social capital, and provide them with the ability to be agents of improvements in their own lives and in the lives of others.

College for America does all of this, and it does not look at all like traditional higher education. In fact, in this new phase in higher education—disaggregated, online, focused on outputs and not inputs—we can rethink not only degree programs, but important learning in areas like civic engagement. In the world of competency-based education, if you say civic learning matters, then the test of that conviction is transparent, straightforward, and rigorous. More importantly, CfA is reaching out to people traditionally excluded from higher education and civic education, and empowering them to have better work, to be full and better citizens, and to have the knowledge and tools to improve their communities.

NOTES

1. For background on this study, see Tamar Lewin, "U.S. Investigating Johns Hopkins Study of Lead Paint Hazard," *New York Times*, August 24, 2001, http://www.nytimes.com/2001/08/24/us/us-investigating-johns-hopkins-study-of-lead-paint-hazard.html.

2. Michael Sandel, *Justice: What's the Right Thing to Do?* (New York: Farrar, Straus, and Giroux, 2009); Sam Harris, "In Defense of Torture," *Huffington Post*, October 17, 2005, http://www.huffingtonpost.com/sam-harris/in-defense-of-torture_b_8993.html.

3. See Dan W. Butin, *Service Learning in Theory and Practice: The Future of Community Engagement in Higher Education* (New York: Palgrave Macmillan, 2010).

4. See Frederick Hess, "Old School: College's Most Important Trend is the Rise of the Adult Student," *The Atlantic*, September 28, 2011, http://www.theatlantic.com/business/archive/2011/09/old-school-colleges-most-important-trend-is-the-rise-of-the-adult-student/245823.

5. Brown University, "For family violence among adolescents, mattering matters," news release, April 18, 2011, https://news.brown.edu/pressreleases/2011/04/mattering; see also Gregory C. Elliott, Susan M. Cunningham, Melissa Colangelo, and Richard J. Gelles, "Perceived Mattering to the Family and Physical Violence within the Family by Adolescents," *Journal of Family Issues* 32, no. 8 (2011): 1007–29.

Rethinking Higher Education: Olin College of Engineering

5

Richard K. Miller

Established in 1938, the F. W. Olin Foundation developed a wonderful legacy in higher education over more than fifty years. The foundation provided the funding for seventy-eight buildings on fifty-eight university campuses, including many well-known universities like Cornell, Johns Hopkins, the University of Southern California, and Vanderbilt, as well many smaller colleges such as Bates, Macalester, Kenyon, Babson, Harvey Mudd, and the Rose-Hulman Institute. However, the foundation decided in 1997 to suspend their building grants program and consider instead establishing an entirely new institution from the ground up. The members of the foundation were concerned about making a positive difference and had noticed that there was a great deal of unhappiness about the way engineering was taught at the time. After consulting with officials at the National Science Foundation and the Accreditation Board for Engineering and Technology, they concluded that what was needed was not simply a new course or degree program here and there, but a whole new mindset. Therefore, nothing short of establishing an entirely new institution would provide the necessary opportunity.

Before reaching this radical conclusion, the members of the foundation first considered the alternative of giving the money to an existing technical university that was already doing things quite well. In addition, they also considered estab-lishing a new college of engineering within an existing university that did not yet have an engineering program. However, they had concluded that the dominant culture in higher education was the primary factor responsible for resistance to the changes that were needed. So, unless a change in culture could be established, the improvements that were sought were unlikely to be sustained. Starting over provided the best chance of achieving the cultural change they sought.

Concern about engineering education continues to this day, and has become more widespread and better recognized. Symptoms of the underlying problems include the following: (1) less than 5 percent of the bachelor's degrees offered nationally go to students who majored in any kind of engineering; (2) about half of all entering freshmen who choose engineering as a major will not graduate in engineering; and (3) less than 20 percent of all students majoring in engineer-ing are female. In addition, and perhaps of even more importance, the National

Academy of Engineering has identified a list of "missing basics" that new engineering graduates will need in the twenty-first century but that are not adequately taught in our engineering programs today.[1] These include greater abilities in design and creativity, teamwork and interdisciplinary thinking, leadership and entrepreneurial behavior, and a greater understanding of the social, political, and economic context of the projects engineers are called upon to lead.

FOUNDING PRECEPTS

The Olin Foundation recorded its purpose in establishing Olin College and outlined key aspects of its operating principles in a document known as the "Founding Precepts," which declared that "Olin College is intended to be different, not for the mere sake of being different, but to become an important and constant contributor to the advancement of engineering education in America and around the world."[2] This unusual, almost "missionary" purpose sets the college apart from any other that I know. Furthermore, it has been fundamental in attracting the type of faculty and staff necessary to create an innovative institution from a blank slate. These individuals were attracted to a cause greater than personal recognition and by the opportunity to seriously explore sweeping ideas that are typically stifled by layers of faculty governance in traditional institutions.

One of the foundation's greatest fears was that the college would quickly settle into the traditions of mainstream higher education and would lose its appetite for innovation. They resented that it was necessary literally to start over in order to enable fundamental change to occur. In an attempt to address this fear, the "Founding Precepts" require that Olin College not provide traditional tenure to its faculty. In addition, the college must always strive to provide full tuition scholarships to all admitted students based on merit, independent of family income. Furthermore, the college must always embrace the principles of continuous improvement and change. As the members of the founding leadership team joined the college, they decided to start the college without organizing the faculty in departments by academic discipline. In addition, they embraced the call for continuous improvement quite literally, establishing the concept that there would be no tenure system at Olin. As a result, the college operates under the assumption that every aspect of the college—including the curriculum and the bylaws—has an expiration date.

IN THE BEGINNING: THE PERIOD OF INVENTION

Few people have had the experience of starting an entire institution from scratch. When I joined Olin College, it was not yet a "place." It was only a concept. We had no land, no assets of any kind, no curriculum, no faculty, staff, or students. The college literally consisted of five people: the four directors of the F.W. Olin Foundation and me, the president and first employee. None of the directors was an engineer or had ever worked in higher education, but they had a passion to create an institution that would become a force for innovation in change in higher education. But how, exactly, do you do that? Where do you start?

That early period was filled with adrenaline, ideas, opportunities, and enormous challenges and risk. Many times in the first thirty months the entire project could have failed. For the first eighteen months, the college had neither faculty nor students. In that sense, it wasn't a "college" by any traditional definition. For the next year we recruited about a dozen faculty members, but no students. During this period we followed a deliberate engineering-inspired process of institutional invention that involved four steps: discovery, invention, development, and testing—of all aspects of the institution, including academic programs, admissions, public relations, administration, and governance.

The following year we added another half dozen faculty members and brought thirty special young students to campus as the "Olin Partners." These students did not take any courses, but rather joined the founding faculty and leadership team literally as "partners in invention" to help conduct experiments for a year, to explore what actually worked and what didn't. The partners were asked to try things that we expected to fail, so that we could observe how they fail and determine the effects of these experiences on the students themselves. Of course, you cannot conduct experiments like this if you are teaching students enrolled for course credit, so the students knew they were not making any progress toward their degrees. Instead, they were helping us determine what material and approaches would be most effective, and why. These Olin Partners—fifteen boys and fifteen girls who graduated from high school in the spring of 2001—were all invited to return the following year as freshman to enroll in the college's inaugural class.

It is difficult to overestimate the importance of this Olin Partner Year (OPY). While the decision to incorporate this year of experimentation into the development of our program was improvised in response to unexpected delays in the parallel process of campus construction, the lessons learned from working closely with these students and watching experiments that we expected to fail accelerated our understanding of the true nature of engineering and the extent to which the learning capacity and abilities of students are underestimated in the literature. The OPY—more than any other single decision—is responsible for the unique and successful learning culture that Olin College is now known for.[3]

For example, before the OPY, our founding faculty were pondering fundamental questions, such as "what is an engineer?" and "what does every engineer need to know?" and "what do you remember from your own undergraduate education in engineering?" We were amazed at how little we could remember with clarity about our undergraduate studies, except for one thing—the senior project in which we actually attempted to build something and make it work. We wondered why it was that we were all forced to wait until the senior year to try this, since the experience seemed to have uniformly produced high levels of retention of lessons learned and also increased motivation and contextual understanding. We assumed that it must not be possible to design and build a complex device until after the prerequisite courses in mathematics and natural science that are ubiquitous today.

The OPY provided an ideal opportunity to see what would happen if we disregarded the conventional wisdom about math and science prerequisites, and instead asked the Olin Partners to design, build, and demonstrate a complex device—before they had taken any college courses at all. We asked them to work in small groups and to build a pulse oximeter—a medical device that measures the pulse rate and oxygen content of blood. The teams had five weeks to learn what pulse oximeters are, understand enough about how they work to design one, and then actually build one and test it. Our plan was to end this experiment after five weeks, with a kind of "mercy killing," in which we would end the frustration and confusion of the students and perform a postmortem on how they had approached this and what went wrong. The rules were that the students should start in the library with the patent literature, where they could read the inventor's description. They could ask any questions of faculty and staff, or anyone they want off campus. But they were required to initiate all questions and take the lead in constructing the hardware.

This project, which was among the first we conducted that year, proved extremely enlightening. First, we were surprised to find that the students were able to succeed at this project, and built their own version of a pulse oximeter that we successfully calibrated against a hospital version. Apparently, it isn't necessary to complete two years of advanced calculus and natural science before completing a project of this complexity! (We later concluded that we should have known this, since engineering is a field in which complex devices frequently evolve from ad hoc experimentation. But we were all academics, and we had long indoctrination in the assumptions that underlie the traditional curriculum in engineering.)

But we also observed something that I regard as far more important than the ability of students to succeed in building the device from day one. The team-based learning experience obviously had a profound effect on the students themselves. They had exceeded their own expectations and became very enthusiastic about the study of engineering. There was a palpable "can do" attitude, through which they felt they were capable of changing the world by engineering things that would change the way people live. This attitude of empowerment and adventure was light years away from the student experience that any of us remember from our own undergraduate years. In fact, in my own, I would describe my undergraduate years as layers and layers of "can't do" experiences built on the assumption that no matter how much science and math you have learned, you are still woefully unprepared for even the most modest project involving the design and construction of an actual piece of hardware.

The Olin Partners' attitude of adventure, empowerment, and "can do," which appeared to persist through numerous other experiments that year, seemed to produce a level of self-efficacy and intrinsic motivation that transformed the learning experience for these students. They were enthusiastic about taking on challenges that seemed beyond reach and doing whatever it takes to succeed. The dominant culture that has emerged and characterizes Olin today might be described by this quote from a recent student on campus: "I have never worked this hard in my life, and there is nothing else I would rather be doing!" Personally, I believe that achieving this type of learning culture on any campus is likely to be more important than any of the curricular details.[4]

Through this and many other experiments in 2001–2, we developed a clear picture of the field of engineering as more than a body of knowledge. It is a process, a way of thinking. (Remember that the airplane was invented in a bicycle shop in Ohio, not a physics lab.) The process, which may or may not involve sophisticated mathematics and science, always proceeds as follows: (1) There must be a better way! (2) Well, why don't we try X? (3) OK, let's build one and try it! (4) Why did it fail? Let's find out. (Then, return to step 1.) One major problem is that the study of engineering in most universities contains very little of this process.

Freed from the assumption that engineering is equivalent to developing content knowledge from a predetermined, long list of technical courses, we developed a new definition of the engineer—one that embraces our mission to address the missing basics identified by the National Academy of Engineering and that has the power to transform the learning environment for science, technology, engineering, and mathematics fields in general. According to our definition, an engineer is a person who envisions what has never been, and then does whatever it takes to make it happen.

Note that this definition requires the ability to envision what has never been. Vision and creativity have not been prominent requirements for entrance to engineering schools, even though the desired characteristics of engineering graduates emphasize enhanced abilities to create and to innovate. This raises serious questions about whether we are attracting the right people to the study of engineering today.[5]

After some soul-searching and careful planning, we decided that we must deliberately look for a new kind of engineering student in order to produce the more innovative and entrepreneurial engineer that is needed—and this was not going to happen through the traditional admissions process. As a result, we developed a required on-campus "candidates' weekend" consisting of extensive team-based and individual interviews of all candidates for admission. No student is admitted to Olin without going through one of these weekends and being evaluated for interpersonal abilities, creativity, passion, and a clear vision for what an engineering education will do. The work of Howard Gardner on "multiple intelligences" has been very influential in our thinking.[6] In the thirteen years we have been enrolling students at Olin College, we have become convinced that educating for attitudes, behaviors, and motivations in addition to knowledge is essential to producing successful graduates in engineering—and most likely, in any field. While it is inconvenient to interview all incoming students, the importance of what we gain from the process is of immeasurable importance to the development of the learning culture and the learning outcomes we seek.

Finally, the OPY also convinced us of the fundamental importance of teamwork and cooperation in learning communities. I doubt that we could produce the results we have seen without the emphasis on learning successfully to lead and follow and to work efficiently and productively on small teams with students who have very different interests and backgrounds. It is typical for an Olin student to complete about twenty team projects in the course of their four-year engineering degree. According to employers who have hired them after graduation, Olin graduates stand out for their ability to organize and lead teams toward useful answers to complex problems almost immediately upon arrival. Interviews with employers frequently comment that Olin graduates seem to have substantial work experience when they first arrive.

All these basic concepts became apparent to us in the first three years, before we enrolled or taught any students. The years of invention were extraordinarily important, and provided both insight and confidence to continue to develop a learning model that depends more heavily than most on experiential learning and teamwork.

However, since these early years also included the major tasks of building the entire institution, several parallel projects of equal magnitude were also underway. These included the design and construction of the entire campus at once; the recruitment of faculty who were best suited to this unusual project, and who were willing to work at an institution without tenure, graduate education, or academic departments; the recruitment of students willing to attend a school that literally did not yet exist (and was not yet accredited), while turning down scholarships from the best-known engineering schools in the nation; building a student life program that fully engages students in the creation of their own learning environment, involving a "learning continuum," core values, a student run honor code, and service learning that promotes high levels of civic engagement; building a board of trustees willing to take fiduciary responsibility for this audacious project, although obviously none of them were alumni; developing critical institutional relations with neighboring partner institutions, Wellesley College and Babson College, where our students would need to cross enroll; developing successful media and governmental relations in a state where "payment in lieu of taxes" is the norm, and where obtaining a charter for a new college involves numerous Catch 22–challenges; and finally, developing an operational culture that strikes the right balance between entrepreneurism (i.e., ask for forgiveness, rather than permission) and institutional control, most apparent in budget management and governance interactions. All these parallel projects are equally important, but there simply isn't enough space here to describe the lessons learned.

THE PERIOD OF REALIZATION

The period from the day we taught our first courses in August 2002 until the day we graduated our first class in May 2006 constituted the "period of realization." During this period, we had somehow to incorporate the lessons learned in the invention period in a program (and an institution) that met schedule and budget requirements, was faithful to the new principles and ideas we had discovered, and didn't require unrealistic amounts of work for members of our community. This was a constant challenge. The overwhelming temptation in this period was simply to copy what some other well-known institution was doing, rather than to take the time to consider all the alternatives. We did our best to resist that at every turn. I believe the opportunity to start from a blank slate is not only a rare opportunity (which is much less frequent than once in a lifetime), but also entails an enormous responsibility to rethink the fundamental goals and objectives and develop fresh approaches that avoid the assumptions and limitations of existing programs elsewhere.

The general principle at work in this period was that of project management. In any project, every decision is driven by three competing priorities: (1) quality/performance, (2) cost/budget, and (3) speed/schedule. In the beginning, it is relatively easy to give the highest priority to quality, and imagine that somehow you will be able to work out the budget and schedule later. Then, in the middle, budget concerns begin to arise, forcing compromise with quality concerns. Finally, near the end, schedule concerns tend to dominate, as deadlines loom and students are scheduled to arrive, etc. There are powerful pressures to manage a project like this by emphasizing business metrics, like budget and schedule, because they are easy to measure and because governance boards have fiduciary responsibility. But I believe that, ten years after opening, few will remember how accurate the original budget or schedule was, but everyone will know by then whether the quality of the institution achieved its full potential.

Here is an illustration of this conflict. There are many practical reasons to announce in advance the number of students you will enroll in your first class. This helps in setting budgets and in determining the size of classrooms, teaching staff, etc. But doing this almost always traps you into accepting whatever quality of students you happen to be able to attract as applicants in that first year. It is the quality of that class—not its size—that will ultimately determine the perceived quality of the institution for years to come. Quality people attract other quality people. It is far wiser to set the quality parameters in advance, and then only enroll the number of students who meet the standards, even if it means there are only a few. Eventually, you will become known for quality, and it will be possible to grow the class while maintaining the quality. It is far easier to establish quality as an initial priority than to change the quality (and reputation) later.

THE ROLE OF ENGAGEMENT: STUDENTS, COMMUNITY, AND CIVIC
One of the most fundamental lessons learned in establishing Olin College is the pervasive importance of the role of engagement. The literature on the role of engagement in enhancing student learning is extensive. Student engagement has become a well-established goal for the enhancement of learning and is the basis for the National Survey of Student Engagement.[7] When viewed through this lens, the focus on teamwork and design-based pedagogy fosters very high levels of student engagement. It is widely accepted now that project-based learning generally fosters higher levels of student engagement than lecture-based learning. I now believe that design-based learning fosters even higher levels of student engagement than project-based learning. This is because students must first diagnose the needs and conceive of multiple solutions before settling on a project aimed at developing a solution. This method aims at purpose-driven learning and fosters creativity and intrinsic motivation. For example, a typical student at Olin completes ten to twenty team-based projects before graduation. Participation in so many teams also fosters high levels of engagement with their education. Olin's mission is to "prepare students to become exemplary engineering innovators who recognize needs, design solutions, and engage in creative enterprises for the good of the world." An early required course asks them to identify a group of people whose lives they want to change.

In my view, creativity is the process of generating original ideas and insights. Inventiveness is the process of generating original ideas and insights that have value. Innovation is the process of generating original ideas and insights that have value—and then implementing them in ways that change the lives of people.

A major innovation changes lives so profoundly that few can even remember life before the innovation was introduced. Olin deliberately attempts to produce innovators, as noted by Tony Wagner in *Creating Innovators: The Making of Young People Who Will Change the World.*[8]

Engineering is a problem-solving profession. It requires engagement with a community where problems reside. At Olin, we approach this in two ways. First, all Olin students are required to complete a senior capstone design course in the senior year in which they work for two consecutive semesters with a corporate sponsor on a real engineering problem that the sponsor brings to them. The company pays $50,000 for the opportunity to work with a team of four to six students for the year, and supplies a liaison engineer to work with the team. The students experience what it is like to "be" an engineer in this engagement with a real corporate client.

In addition, the majority of Olin students are involved in service learning in the community. This involves many activities both on and off campus, including courses like Engineering for Humanity, where students and faculty work with a group of local senior citizens to design solutions that improve their daily lives in some way. In addition, Olin students engage in joint courses and collaborative projects with students from neighboring Wellesley College and Babson College that are focused on sustainability in the developing world. Friday afternoons at Olin are set aside for community-service projects, and very few courses are scheduled during this period. While nearly all campuses have activities of this type, at Olin the participation by all students is remarkable.

Finally, Olin has developed a level of global engagement that is rare for an undergraduate institution. In addition to the usual emphasis on study abroad (about 25 percent of Olin students complete such an experience) and hosting of exchange students from abroad, Olin has hosted visits from faculty and administrators from more than two hundred universities since 2010. The majority of these visitors are from other nations. These visitors have identified Olin as an unusual institution with a learning culture that is of particular interest, and they hope to learn how they might benefit from our experimental program. This is because, as previously noted, Olin's "Founding Precepts" require us to attempt to contribute to the advancement of engineering education in America and throughout the world. We do this now by working with groups of like-minded faculty from institutions around the world who attend our summer institute on the development of more effective learning methods. Since no two institutions are alike, our approach involves consultation and co-design efforts—not duplication of Olin courses—at other institutions, a process in which our experienced faculty members facilitate workshops where visitors work in small groups to develop their own experimental learning projects. The key ideas of student engagement, teamwork, intrinsic motivation, and design thinking are pervasive, but each visitor leaves with a unique vision of how these concepts may be applied in the context of their home institution. As a result, Olin has a series of many institutional engagements of varying intensity throughout the world.

> *Engagement with others and with the grand challenges of our age is the most effective way to enhance learning*

An illustration of the global vision of Olin College is provided by the leadership role we have taken in focusing global attention on the Grand Challenges of the 21st Century, a list of fundamental complex challenges facing humanity identified by the US National Academy of Engineering. The challenges may be grouped into four major categories: security, sustainability, health, and enhancing life. Nearly all young people—whether they are interested in engineering or not—are concerned about these challenges. The challenges help foster a personal goal and purpose for education. They have the power to attract young people into the study and resolution of problems that are much bigger than personal recognition or wealth. With this realization, Olin has partnered with Duke University and the University of Southern California in organizing two national summits on the Grand Challenges and the first International Summit on the Grand Challenges, which was held in London in March 2013. Furthermore, together with our two partners, we developed the Grand Challenge Scholars Program, in which undergraduate engineering students at any university may receive personal recognition from the National Academy of Engineering for completing a program of extracurricular activity in five areas involving service learning, international study, interdisciplinary study, a project on one of the Grand Challenges, and a project involving entrepreneurship. Last year, the proportion of Olin's student body that completed the Grand Challenge Scholars Program was the highest of any of the many participating universities.

I am convinced that engagement with others and with the grand challenges of our age is the most effective way to enhance learning and improve educational outcomes for our students. Of course, the results of this type of engagement also promise to produce graduates who are better citizens and institutions that are better integrated into their communities.

NOTES

1. National Academy of Engineering, *The Engineer of 2020: Visions of Engineering in the New Century* (Washington, DC: National Academies Press, 2004).

2. "Statement of Founding Precepts for Franklin W. Olin College of Engineering," Olin College, accessed February 9, 2014, http://www.olin.edu/sites/default/files/olin_founding-precepts.pdf.

3. The Olin learning model was selected for the 2013 Bernard M. Gordon Prize for Innovation in Engineering and Technology Education by the US National Academy of Engineering, a $500,000 award that is regarded as the nation's highest recognition for innovation in this field.

4. Independent evidence of this unique learning culture is provided by recent national surveys conducted by the Princeton Review that identified Olin College as one of the top ten universities in the United States where "student study the most," but also where "students are the happiest." The Princeton Review, *The Best 378 Colleges*, (Framingham, MA: TPR Education IP Holdings, 2014), 38–42. I don't know of any other technical college or university that has been ranked in these two categories simultaneously. Charles Vest, former president of MIT and of the US National Academy of Engineering recently explained that "making universities and engineering schools exciting, creative, adventurous, rigorous, demanding, and empowering milieus is more important than specifying curricular details." Vest, "Educating Engineers for 2020 and Beyond," *The Bridge* 36, no. 2 (2006): 38–44.

5. Most engineering students today will tell you that they were pointed toward the study of engineering by their high school counselors because they were good at math and natural science courses, not because they were creative or had skills in project management.

6. See, for example, Howard Gardner, *Multiple Intelligences: New Horizons in Theory and Practice* (New York: Basic Books, 1993).
7. See http://nsse.iub.edu.
8. Tony Wagner, *Creating Innovators: The Making of Young People Who Will Change the World* (New York: Scribner, 2012).

6 | Value Studies and Democratic Citizenship

Peter Hajnal and Thomas Nørgaard

A Brief Introduction to Value Studies

"Value studies" refers to a form of liberal education developed at the European College of Liberal Arts (ECLA) in Berlin between 2003 and 2012. Based on this curricular approach, ECLA introduced its first degree program in 2009 and was formally recognized as a German university in 2011. The first cohort of students received their bachelor of arts degree in value studies in 2012. Our aim in this essay is to explain how the value studies curriculum honors and promotes ideals of democratic citizenship. But first, we present a brief sketch of the curriculum.

As the name suggests, value studies is a curriculum focused on questions about values. In an institution without departments, students work with faculty from a variety of academic backgrounds on moral, political, economic, epistemic, religious, and aesthetic questions with the understanding that such questions are naturally and deeply connected. While students read and write a great deal, often reflect in solitude, and occasionally listen to lectures, the central activity supported by the curriculum is conversation in small seminars and tutorials.

The assumed connectedness of our questions about values is the first of four basic premises behind the curriculum. When studying ethics, we easily end up thinking about political or religious questions. An epistemic question may turn out to have an inescapable aesthetic aspect. Since the various issues on the table tend to be intimately connected, a value studies curriculum is by definition heavily integrated. The most natural way to ensure integration is to build up the curriculum around core courses that secure the relevant breadth and cohesion.

The second premise is that the most fundamental questions about values have a claim on us as human beings—no matter what we take a special interest in, and no matter what we do for a living. But we tend to specialize in values, to focus on a few and more or less lose sight of the rest. Sometimes this is as it should be, but often we miss out on the fullness of life to the detriment of ourselves and others. The demands of the moment, habit, anxiety, and selfishness may shrink a person's world to a caricature of what it could be. Nicolai Hartmann, one of the thinkers whose work has been an inspiration for the development of value studies, thought that this is the common destiny of human beings. "The tragedy of man," he once wrote, "is that of one who, sitting at a well-laden table, is hungry but who will not reach out his hand, because he does not see what is before him."[1] There is enough truth in this dark yet also optimistic thought to justify a course of study that strives to combat our natural narrowness.

Value questions remain primarily "human" even in an academic context. This is the third premise. While values lend themselves to study—eminently so—no discipline, understood as a set of methods or a body of literature, can tame or appropriate them. The values of justice, beauty, and natural diversity are all studied fruitfully by experts in various contexts, for example, but their significance is pre-disciplinary and remains anchored in ordinary human life, even when addressed by academics. For that reason, the primary task of scholars dedicated to value studies is not to pursue or represent their respective disciplines, but to bring whatever expertise they have to bear on questions of general human significance.

The fourth and final premise is the most difficult to articulate, but important nonetheless. When we talk about "values," we have in mind the goods, ends, and ideals by which we understand who we are and explain what we do. Values tend to be deeply personal, yet typically not just private. They often come into our purview as shared objects of attention and, at least to some extent, as fitting objects of reasoned conversation. In fact, they commonly seem to *call out* for conversation. As creatures who value—wonder, cherish, and desire—we need an intimate yet open social space where we can talk together, a hall of joint and living reflection. Conversation, in other words, is one of the natural expressions of our many responses to things of value and meaningful experience: bafflement, bliss, ambivalence, frustration, anxiety. There is a crucial educational aspect to such conversation. It is, among other things, a conversation that each generation owes the next. To some extent it happens informally in families and among friends, and this is of immense importance; but in these contexts the conversation often remains too sporadic, too superficial, too private, or too one-sided to do full justice to the task. That's why we need value studies.

SELF-KNOWLEDGE, REFLECTION, AND CIVILITY

The ultimate educational ends of value studies are plural, and to some extent essentially open and contested. This is as it should be. It would be illiberal and counterproductive to assume that we could posit the *telos* of this sort of educational journey from the beginning. Nonetheless, one ideal outcome, arguably, is a deepened or refined self-knowledge. This is a personal good, but here it is important to point out that it is a civic good also. As Jean Bethke Elshtain wrote in a previous volume in the Civic Series, "people propel themselves into community and organizational life because there are things they care about, values they endorse, goods they embrace."[2] For most of us, most of the time, knowing who we are and what we care about makes us more meaningfully and sure-footedly engaged in civic and political life. A striking confirmation of this thought may be found in the important work of Adam Davis, in whose Civic Reflection Project we see a sister of value studies.[3]

Some might worry whether a course of study that defines itself by reference to values must in some manner take the form of indoctrination. The worry is fair enough; but it is neither specific to value studies, nor is it possible to overcome entirely in any form of education. Even studies that look purely instrumental or technical in character will involve value commitments. Implicitly or explicitly, every curriculum reveals a sense of relevance and an ideal of learning. The precise identification of these commitments may be difficult, but complete neutrality is impossible. Furthermore, there is no good reason to think that an explicit focus on values must be associated with some special bias or dogmatic modes of teaching. On the contrary, an explicit curricular focus on values may, under the right circumstances, inspire a reflectiveness that makes the educational endeavor less likely to be indoctrinatory.

In the *Euthyphro,* Plato had Socrates point out that disagreement about values—about "right and wrong, and noble and disgraceful, and good and bad"—is a common source of anger and enmity.[4] This fact may sometimes be, or seem to be, a compelling reason for avoiding discussions about values. Some liberals, for example, dream of a neutral polity that would not commit a community to any substantial notion of the good life. Some academics pursue "value-free" science, and some educators seek to banish politics from their classrooms. Value studies is premised on the opposite thought: we cannot avoid substantial value commitments (or disagreements) in politics, science, and education, and we are often better off facing them with as much candor as we can muster. In fact, the confrontations that emerge from such conversations often have profound educational value. As we work through them, we achieve reflective depth and have occasion to practice a number of intellectual and civic virtues of great significance, not least in a democracy.

Of the various virtues needed to sustain a conversation about values, civility may be one of the most central. In a minimal sense, it marks our ability to maintain a basic respect and exhibit tolerance even when we disapprove of another person's behavior or opinions. Civility in this sense, on occasion necessary in any public and genuine conversation about values, is probably a norm of behavior that no democratic community can do without.

The term "civility" has another usage, however, according to which it is not merely a last resort in the effort of maintaining our community in the face of disagreement, but an expression of something more positive and more ambitious. As Robert Pippin suggests, civility may be understood as "as an active attempt to recognize and help to promote each other as free beings."[5] While a democracy could perhaps exist without this sort of civility, one may nonetheless think of it as a profound democratic ideal, as expressing a substantial and optimistic sense of equality and solidarity. The darkest moments of political life may seem to condemn this ideal as utopian; but if we believe that some utopias should be kept on the map somehow, we might want to design some of our curricula to promote exactly that sort of civility. Value studies does that. When we foreground and face disagreements, we may also reveal deeper commonalities or discover new possibilities of harmonious diversity. In other words, while joint explorations of the good, the true, and the beautiful may reveal terrible human dilemmas and political dynamite of the most destructive kind, they are not divisive by definition. They do not just reveal the limits of freedom in a democracy, but may help us push those limits a bit. We learn that the battle for freedom is not simply a zero-sum game. Since we don't know where the limits of collective freedom lie, hope is a civic virtue closely related to civility. The study of values keeps that hope alive and helps us prevent politics from being a sphere that simply belongs to fate.

Discipline, Expertise, and Wisdom

The value studies curriculum was not designed to facilitate what we call "disciplinary training": the command of a certain body of literature, a special set of methods, and one particular mode of thinking. Like other curricular innovations from the past century, value studies is meant to complement the one-sided dominance of disciplines in higher education. Many of us, even when grateful for the rigorous disciplinary training we have received, have experienced how the disciplinary approach to learning may become self-serving and almost hide from view the human ends and issues for which most of us awoke to the life of learning in the first place. Arguably, this danger of losing one's ends is inherent to disciplinary training. To be alive to fundamental questions about human ends in all their complexity is the first business of value studies; the second is to make some sort of progress with them. There are competing conceptions of what this progress consists in, and that is as it should be. The main point here is that the insistence on staying with an issue, problem, or question of fundamental human relevance involves a certain concentration and persistence that can only be understood as a form of *discipline* in the everyday sense of that word—a capacity for focus, patience, and constancy of purpose. Moreover, this sort of discipline is not just a private good, but a civic virtue. A democracy needs citizens with a strong and not easily diverted sense of the goods and ideals for which we do everything we do.

> *A democracy needs citizens with a not easily diverted sense of goods and ideals*

The focus on values fosters a deep sense of equality in the classroom. The most fundamental issues raised are those to which all human beings by virtue of their ordinary experience have some form of "privileged access." At no moment in a conversation about values can it be ruled out that the most interesting or fruitful contribution will come from a participant who is theoretically the least prepared. Sometimes our most important questions are the ones that look simplistic or obvious. It does not follow that expertise is irrelevant. On the contrary, our discussions about values constantly benefit from expert knowledge—about literature, history, religion, anthropology, economics, statistics, technology, science, and other subjects. Being well-informed is a good thing, and a student may well be inspired by value studies to acquire and live by a certain expertise, practical or scholarly. What we learn from value studies is "simply" that the last word on fundamental human issues does not belong to the expert.

This lesson should inspire us with the courage to ask innocent questions. It should also help us overcome, as far as possible, our tendencies to snobbism, pedantry, and theoretical arrogance. The implication is that those who teach value studies must do without the kind of authority that is guaranteed at other places of higher learning by departmental structure and students' ability to choose as their goal of study a discipline that their teachers have already mastered. They nonetheless earn respect, if they are good, as knowledgeable and imaginative designers of syllabi, as attentive and inspiring teachers, and—ideally—as possessing a little of that human quality for which there is no better name than "wisdom." As A. N. Whitehead wrote in *The Aims of Education,* "wisdom is the way in which knowledge is held. It concerns the handling of knowledge, its selection for the determination of relevant issues, its employment to add value to our immediate experience. This mastery of knowledge, which is wisdom, is the most intimate freedom obtainable."[6]

EQUALITY, HUMILITY, AND SOLIDARITY

Value studies is essentially a democratic form of education. This curriculum is partially built around a deep sense of human equality, and it honors virtues that are crucial for democratic citizenship. That's what we have been trying to argue so far. It is important to see, however, that the curriculum is not *fanatically* democratic; it is not closed to everything that does not bear a clear democratic stamp. While some democratic educators are intolerant of anything that challenges their democratic ideals, value studies allows us, nay *invites* us, to ask hard questions about our favored polity. As one of the most profound and sovereign ideals of our time, democracy itself is an obvious topic for a value studies curriculum.

Back in 1923, Whitehead asked a hard question about equality as the central value in the complex ideal of democracy. "We are at the threshold of a democratic age," he wrote, "and it remains to be determined whether the equality of man is to be realised on a high level or a low level."[7] This statement might be a good starting point for a seminar discussion at ECLA. It invites a principled discussion about the metaphors of high and low—that is, the nature and significance of hierarchical thinking. It may also provoke the egalitarian to think hard about his attachment to equality: what exactly am I committed to? Even firmly committed democrats should be able to ponder the question, or questions, behind this statement. No doubt, some will be tempted by this occasion to think antidemocratic thoughts, but others might be inspired to deepen their understanding of and attachment to the democratic ideal. Whitehead's statement does not necessarily express the worries of a crypto-elitist. It may express a sense of human dignity that is deeply solidaristic. And it may suggest a worried question about the future of democracy: if we do not manage to realize human equality on a fairly high level, will the human race survive, and will it survive with its dignity intact? Arguably, now when the democratic age is well on its way, this question remains unanswered.

Not only would Whitehead's statement be a helpful starting point for an ECLA seminar, but it also provides a natural starting point for our final point about the significance of value studies for democratic citizenship. In order to make this point, let us develop the thoughts of the worried democrat a bit further. In this mood, we may feel a somber ambivalence about the concept of equality, as if it were a magnificent ship with a malignant stowaway. The belief that all human beings are equal has a tendency to bring with it another: the belief that every desire and satisfaction of every equal being must be equal too. Push-pin is as good as poetry, not because we have judged them to be equally good, but because there can be no judgment to make.

Who am I to judge? And who can judge me? In other words, noble egalitarianism leads many of us to (flirt with) shallow relativism. The common result, one might fear, is a character too timid to discriminate at all and defiantly proud of his own taste, whatever it happens to be. A version of Whitehead's low realization of equality could be a "democratic" society inhabited by such persons. Because they lack humility and confidence, it would be a "formal" democracy suffering from a lack of individual aspiration and civic apathy—all in the name of a misguided sense of equality.

Our own mood is not always so dark, but the danger apprehended in that mood seems real enough. The democratic danger, if we may call it that, has particular sting in modern life. Modern life has many acute observers, but for our purposes Nicolai Hartmann is particularly helpful again:

> The life of man to-day is not favourable to depth of insight. The quiet and contemplation are lacking, life is restless and hurried; there is competition, aimless and without reflection. Whoever stands still for a moment is overtaken by the next. And as the claims of the outer life chase one another, so likewise do the impressions, experiences and sensations. We are always looking out for what is newest, the last thing continuously governs us and the thing before the last is forgotten ere it has been fairly seen, much less comprehended. We live from sensation to sensation. And our penetration becomes shallow, our sense of value is blunted, by snatching at the sensational. Not only is modern man restless and precipitate, dulled and blasé, but nothing inspires, touches, lays hold of his innermost being. Finally he has only an ironical and weary smile for everything. Yes, in the end he makes a virtue of his moral degradation. He elevates the *nil admirari,* his incapacity to feel wonder, amazement, enthusiasm and reverence, into a planned habit of life. Callously passing lightly over everything is a comfortable *modus vivendi.* And thus he is pleased with himself in a pose of superiority which hides his inner vacuity.[8]

The modern democratic person lives a dangerous life. It is all too easy for us to become proud, diffident, and restlessly apathetic. Some respond to this problem with denial, others with despair. Some become reactionaries or secretly begin to despise democracy. Value studies is meant to help us avoid these temptations. It is, among other things, a democratic and optimistic antidote to a democratic disease. It is a curriculum that invites students and teachers to the joint and solidaristic pursuit of high-minded equality.

Notes

1. Nicolai Hartmann, *Ethics*, trans. Stanton Colt (London: G. Allen & Unwin Ltd., 1932), 39.
2. Jean Bethke Elshtain, "The Moral Imperatives of Civic Life" in *Civic Values, Civic Practices,* ed. Donald W. Harward (Washington, DC: Bringing Theory to Practice, 2013), 47.
3. For information about the Civic Reflection Project, see http://www.civicreflection.org/.
4. Plato, *Euthyphro. Apology. Crito. Phaedo. Phaedrus,* trans. Harold North Fowler, Loeb Classical Library 36 (Cambridge, MA: Harvard University Press, 1914), 27.
5. Robert Pippin, *The Ethical Status of Civility in the Persistence of Subjectivity: On the Kantian Aftermath* (New York: Cambridge University Press, 2005), 237.
6. A. N. Whitehead, *The Aims of Education and Other Essays* (New York: The Free Press, 1967), 30.
7. Ibid., 69.
8. Hartmann, *Ethics,* 44–45.

PART 2 | Civic Perspectives
and Strategies

Building a University-Wide College of Citizenship and Public Service

Robert M. Hollister

i

IN 2000, AS PART OF AN AMBITIOUS UNIVERSITY-WIDE CIVIC EDUCATION initiative designed to educate students in all fields for lifetimes of active citizenship, Tufts University established the Tisch College of Citizenship and Public Service. Through an aggressive interdisciplinary approach, the university aimed to develop citizen engineers, citizen physicians, and citizen businessmen and women—people who are highly competent in their chosen professional fields and who also have in abundance the values and skills needed to be effective agents of change in their communities. Rather than giving a separate degree, the college serves as a catalyst and a resource to all parts of the university in order to help faculty and students in all disciplines integrate active citizenship into curricular, extracurricular, and other programs.

Embarking on a campaign of culture change intended to make "active citizenship" a defining part of the institution's ethos, we have advanced civic education in all parts of the institution through extensive programs of faculty support, student leadership development, community partnerships, and alumni activities.

With substantial institutional commitment, ample financial support, and strong collective leadership from multiple constituencies of the university, Tufts has made steady progress toward its ambitious goal. Today, in 2013, "active citizenship" is a defining part of the university's identity. A growing portion of students in diverse fields are graduating with the values and skills they need in order to be effective leaders for change. Each year, over one hundred undergraduates graduate with *honos civicus* ("civic honors"), a recognition of their substantive academic and extracurricular achievement; many times that number of graduating seniors have gained substantial civic skills and knowledge through multiple courses, extracurricular experiences, and internships. The medical school now requires all students to complete at least fifty hours of voluntary community service. And each of the other professional schools has taken steps to reinforce civic education as a defining dimension of their degrees. An endowment gift of $40 million from alumnus Jonathan Tisch has provided a strong financial foundation.

What strategies and other factors have enabled Tufts to make the progress that it has made to date? As founding dean of Tisch College, I believe we have had success with the approaches described below.

AVOID THE PUBLIC SERVICE AS "THIRD MISSION" TRAP

To date, most proponents of the civic renewal of higher education have stayed within the paradigm of public service as the "third mission" of the university. They advocate that public service functions should receive greater attention and support than they currently do, in comparison with teaching and research missions.

Our experience at Tufts suggests that this "third mission" focus is a trap. Teaching and research always will be the primary missions of a university. It is wishful thinking to suggest that public service as a separate endeavor can secure anywhere near the same level of support as the two primary missions. An alternative approach is to frame civic engagement as a route to higher quality teaching and research, to elevate civic engagement as an important dimension of teaching and research, to grow community-engaged teaching and research, and to demonstrate that community engagement can achieve higher quality teaching and research.

The experience of Tufts Civil and Environmental Engineering Professor Chris Swan provides an example of this alternative approach. Professor Swan became a passionate advocate of community service learning after the College of Citizenship and Public Service helped him add a team service project to his course on soil remediation. Subsequently, he began to tell his engineering colleagues, "Not only did my students start to gain civic skills, they learned the technical concepts and methods better and faster." Professor Swan went on to win two National Science Foundation grants for comparative studies of the learning outcomes produced by alternative approaches to community service learning in engineering programs. For this professor community service activities embedded in his courses have had a positive effect on community conditions, and they have enhanced his teaching and opened up major new research opportunities as well.

CONCENTRATE ON BUILDING FACULTY LEADERSHIP

A cornerstone of our approach has been to invest heavily in building faculty leadership—to develop professors' capabilities in community-engaged teaching and research, and also to encourage and support them as leaders driving and refining our plan. Those faculty members who are integrating active citizenship into their courses and their research are the invisible faculty of the college. With primary academic appointments in their home departments and schools, they hold secondary academic appointments in Tisch College that recognize and support their contributions and responsibilities to the collective effort that cuts across departmental and school silos.

We have found especially effective a faculty fellows program that each year selects ten to twelve professors from diverse fields to pursue civic engagement curriculum development and research projects. Selected through a competitive process, the faculty fellows meet monthly and receive financial and staff support for their individual projects, which are designed to build active citizenship throughout the institution. The fellows program has built a widening circle of faculty members who are leading civic education and scholarship in all schools. They constitute a growing intellectual community of shared interest and commitment to active citizenship.

A few years into the process of developing Tisch College, faculty began really to own it and to take responsibility for much of the programming. Their independent initiative and active partnership in building active citizenship across Tufts has been a key ingredient. For example, as a faculty fellow of the college, Professor Doug Brugge of the medical school organized an effort to develop university-community collaboration on research. He developed the Tufts Community Research Center, which is governed by a board with equal representation of Tufts academics and host community representatives. The center identifies and nurtures community-engaged research, and it has played a pivotal role in landing major grants for projects that have been planned and also implemented by both academic and community colleagues.

EMBRACE AND FOSTER DEBATE ABOUT CIVIC GOALS AND STRATEGIES
In order to renew its civic mission, any given institution of higher education does not need to embrace a single, unified vision. While the majority of Tufts faculty readily supported Tisch College and its bold plans, there were also some critics. While we, of course, have needed a substantial base of support, our approach has been to welcome critical dialogue as well, on questions such as the following: Should civic values include challenging established structure of power and privilege? Should the civic capabilities we teach include skills for protest and revolution? In order effectively to renew their civic missions, colleges and universities do need to mobilize sufficient internal support for their plans, but they also would do well to foster high-quality debate about civic values and institutional roles. That should be a significant part of their civic vision.

One day, when I asked the chair of the English Department for his support, he said, "Our role isn't to support your effort; rather, it is to critically interrogate it—to explore the contradictions and negative assumptions that are built into your vision." On another occasion, Jonathan Wilson, a highly accomplished professor of English, was slated to deliver the faculty talk at the annual PhD hooding ceremony for the Graduate School of Arts and Sciences. He approached me right beforehand and said, "I hope you won't be offended, but my talk will focus on the virtues of 'inactive citizenship.'" In his speech, he argued that it was as worthy for a student to spend her summer studying and writing poetry as it was to work for a local community organization. And, of course, he is right; it is not an either-or proposition. I appreciated his sensitivity, but immediately was delighted with his critical talk. It was interesting and provocative, and I knew right away that this was a significant indicator that Tisch College had arrived. We had succeeded in framing the debate. "Active citizenship" had gained real traction in our academic culture.

PARTICIPATE IN, AND CONTRIBUTE TO, OUR COLLECTIVE MOVEMENT
As we began our initiative in the late 1990s, we benefitted immensely from the experience of, and guidance from, sister institutions. Ira Harkavy was an especially

generous source of advice and encouragement.[1] We have learned regularly from the experience of other universities, such as Michigan State's pioneering efforts in the areas of faculty assessment and tenure and promotion criteria and the University of California–Los Angeles's "UCLA in LA" grants program for university-community collaborative projects. We rediscovered the power of external validation in higher education. When advocating various policy changes to advance civic education at Tufts, on several occasions it has been very helpful to be able to say, "This isn't a wild idea; they already have been doing it for several years at the University of North Carolina and the University of Minnesota, and here are the results."

All of us who are building civic education efforts in our respective institutions have an opportunity and a responsibility to support each other's work and to grow our movement. At Tufts, we have initiated two networks that are vehicles for us to learn from others and also to share our experience with them. Because all of us in academia work for organizations that vigorously resist change, we need interinstitutional support in order to dismantle our individual ivory towers. In 2005, together with Campus Compact,[2] we invited the heads of thirteen civic engagement programs at research universities across the United States to spend a weekend together sharing their experiences and visions. The group formed an ongoing alliance, The Research University Civic Engagement Network, that has been meeting annually ever since. Campus Compact has served very effectively as secretariat for the network, whose membership has grown to include over thirty-five institutions.

Also in 2005, Tufts invited twenty-nine heads of universities from twenty-three countries to the university's conference center in Talloires, France, to share their civic engagement experiences and dreams. It was such a timely and energizing conversation that the group formed the Talloires Network and prevailed upon Tufts to provide secretariat support. Since the founding conference, the Talloires Network has grown to include over three hundred universities in seventy-two counties with a combined student of enrollment of over six million. It has become the primary global coalition of engaged universities. Members exchange best practices and collaborate to elevate support from public and private funders. In the process, we strengthen civic engagement at our own universities and also at sister institutions around the world.

NOTES
1. Ira Harkavy is associate vice president and founding dean of the Barbara and Edward Netter Center for Community Partnerships at the University of Pennsylvania.
2. Campus Compact is a national coalition of over 1,100 college and university presidents committed to civic education.

Civic Diffusion: Moving the Center to the Center

ii

Darby K. Ray

ONE SIGN OF THE PUTATIVE SUCCESS of the higher education civic engagement movement of the past twenty or so years is the presence on many campuses of a center, institute, or office dedicated to service learning, community partnerships, public engagement, social change, and/or engaged democracy. Such centers, institutes, and offices are widely understood to signal serious institutional commitment to civic learning and action.[1] As such, they often appear prominently in recruitment materials, on college and university websites, and in applications for the Carnegie Community Engagement Classification and other forms of institutional recognition.

Notwithstanding the complex labors that produce and sustain centers of engagement and the significant impact their sponsored programs and staff often have on student learning and development, campus cultures, off-campus communities, and diverse fields of knowledge and practice, we might pause to ask whether, in centering the civic in a center, we unwittingly marginalize the civic and undermine its full emancipatory potential. Centers, after all, tend to exist in a kind of no-man's-land, neither fully curricular nor fully cocurricular and, hence, often without the kind of intimate understanding, full-bodied support, or connectional networks enjoyed by other institutional entities. More to the point, when the civic is identified with a center, do we risk letting the rest of the campus off the hook—making it somehow less responsible for civic learning and action because such things are perceived to be the purview of the center? Or, do those of us who work in or relate to centers or offices of engagement let *ourselves* off the hook by framing our work primarily in programmatic rather than institutional terms?[2]

What would it mean to bring the civic to the center of institutional life, and what role could centers, institutes, and offices play in such a strategic relocation? While specific strategies would vary with institutional contexts, the tendency of the civic to become siloed in one campus entity would be counteracted if centers were to exert intentionally centripetal forces, directing energy not only toward college-community partnerships, but also, and with equal intentionality and imagination, toward the strengthening of civility and relationships of mutual transformation among *on-campus* departments, programs, offices, and constituencies.

Most campuses are as needful of internal partnership building as they are of authentic off-campus connections. Indeed, higher education institutions will not fulfill their potential for inspired and effective public engagement unless and until internal networks of connection and collaboration are healed and grown. For those of us within engagement centers or offices, this work calls for both humility and magnanimity, for both self-critique and radical hospitality—importantly, the same postures and practices we seek to embody as we engage the off-campus world.

On some campuses, humility might involve the realization that in our zeal for developing definitions, rubrics, and best practices intended to create an identifiable field of community-engaged inquiry and action and to inspire excellence in both inputs and outcomes, we may be excluding, devaluing, delimiting, or refusing to see important work being done by others on the campus. Might it be possible to adopt a more expansive model of engagement—the civic as a continuum, for example, or better yet, the civic as a dynamic cycle of learning and action that invites a wide range of perspectives and practices? Many have labored long and hard to shift both the theory and practice of engagement from a one-way or patronage model to a two-way or partnership model in which collaboration, co-creation, and mutual transformation are the guiding aims and principles. Could we sustain these important gains while also broadening our understanding of what "counts" as the civic at our institutions? When our centers and institutes function less as gatekeepers or scorekeepers and more as gracious hosts, our invitations attract new campus allies and prospective partners, some of whose work may challenge current definitions and categories of engagement.

The civic as a defining institutional priority that reaches well beyond the confines of a center, institute, or office means that civic learning and action are not only mission-statement intentions but also mission-critical values that are operationalized throughout the college or university. The infusion of the civic can occur along a variety of trajectories and with appeals to differently perceived goods. For example, since institutional mission statements increasingly claim civic intentions, such statements can be used strategically to encourage civic buy-in from a wide range of institutional players—especially senior staff members and trustees, who are accustomed to thinking in terms of broad institutional goals and claims. In like fashion, certain faculty and staff members may be more persuaded by arguments that appeal to institution-focused goods than by arguments that appeal to broader goods, like social justice or community well-being. Even if high-level affirmations of the civic are, in reality, primarily rhetorical or proleptic, they can nevertheless be used strategically to move institutional players toward greater investment in them. Because such statements have already secured institutional approval at the highest levels, they can be invoked with authority by advocates of civic learning and action. When we do this in good faith, we can often move institutional leaders from purely theoretical affirmations to concrete support for practical enactments of civic mission. Reminding our leaders that civic learning and leadership are constitutive of institutional identity and productive of institutional goods gives them compelling internal reasons to invest in such work.

Another important leverage point for moving the civic to the center of our colleges and universities is student learning. Some faculty teach in fields with readily acknowledged and even expected links to public engagement; other faculty have strong internal motivations or are fortunate to work at institutions with good faculty incentive and reward programs related to civically engaged teaching, service, or scholarship. But to one degree or another, all faculty care about or work toward student learning, and for them the civic can be compelling pedagogical terrain. Underscoring its inclusion in oft-cited lists of high-impact learning practices, we might pause to consider that one way of conceiving of the civic is as a space where the learner and the thing to be learned—the knower and the known—encounter each other in mutual openness or discovery.[3] The civic is not a neutral space; it is a shared space whose premise is hospitality, an invitation to encounter the other with authenticity and respect, a desire to inhabit a world where both self and other can flourish.

In learning, the learner encounters an other—for example, an idea, an argument, a painting, an organism, a landscape, a person, a language, or a culture—and the learner is changed as a result of this encounter. True learning pulls the learner out of him or herself, out of the world as s/he knows it, and into a new, broader space constituted by the mutual engagement of knower and known. To learn is to step into uncharted territory such that the distance between knower and known is lessened and some bit of shared space, which we call understanding, comes into being. Learning and the civic, then, share a similar dynamic. Civic engagement *is* bridge building for the sake of authentic understanding. We move the civic to the center of our institutions when institutes and centers of engagement articulate and incarnate the shared intentions and structures of deep learning and the civic—the risk taking and bridge building they each undertake for the sake of understanding.

When the civic is embraced as a space of deep learning, its centrality to the mission of higher education is underscored. At the same time, the possibilities for its purposeful diffusion throughout the institution become apparent. After all, world-expanding, bridge-building encounters with the unfamiliar, different, or unknown can happen almost anywhere. Community-engaged learning courses and research projects co-created by college and community partners are certainly one such site, but they do not exhaust the possibilities.

If the civic is not a single destination or practice but rather the embodiment of connected learning in pursuit of shared goods, then the pathways toward its actualization are limited only by the imagination and the will. Wherever students are is where the civic can be instantiated. For many institutions, residence halls are places of untapped civic promise, whether through institutionally supported experiments in shared governance, publicly engaged learning communities, or any number of other bridge-building initiatives. Athletics, too, can be fruitful ground for civic cultivation. The athlete-coach relationship is often one of the most formative for students, so growing the civic understanding and investment of coaches is a key strategy for operationalizing an institution's civic mission. Similarly, student clubs and organizations are important spawning grounds for leadership development and peer norming, and yet they tend on many campuses to be only sporadically mobilized for civic action.

More systematic investment in the civic can also be cultivated by working with leaders in student government to build support for campus-wide systems of engagement—for example, by establishing a "community liaison" position on the slate of officers required for a student organization to gain institutional recognition and funding eligibility. Increasingly, we are realizing the vital links between civic engagement initiatives and the flourishing of first-generation college students, students of color, and other students from groups traditionally under-represented in higher education.[4] Establishing strong and sustainable connections between the diversity/equity work and the community engagement work taking place on our campuses is yet another way the civic can begin to pervade our institutions. Similar connections can be made to environmental sustainability work and to wellness initiatives.

When centers, institutes, and offices of engagement become forces of centripetal energy and radical hospitality, the possibilities for "sharing" the civic with others across the college or university are multitudinous. Ironically, as we put civic engagement into practice in our own institutions—focusing less on the center, institute, or office and more on the challenges and joys of cultivating civic learning and action among diverse partners on our own campuses—we may well find ourselves better equipped, and in better company, to lead our institutions in deep engagements of off-campus communities.

Notes

1. For recent work on centers, see Carole A. Beere, James C. Votruba, and Gail W. Wells, *Becoming an Engaged Campus: A Practical Guide for Institutionalizing Public Engagement* (San Francisco: Jossey-Bass, 2011); and Ariane Hoy and Mathew Johnson, eds., *Deepening Community Engagement in Higher Education: Forging New Pathways* (New York: Palgrave Macmillan, 2013).

2. An even more radical query, worth pursuing on its own and hence not the focus of this essay, is the question of whether higher education's institutionalization of the civic via the service learning/civic engagement "movement" signals or contributes to the cooptation or erasure of that very movement by directing activist energies and resources toward institutional ends instead of larger goods. See Mavis Morton, Corey Dolgon, Timothy Maher, and James Pennell, "Civic Engagement and Public Sociology: Two 'Movements' in Search of a Mission," *Journal of Applied Social Science* 6, no. 1 (2012) 5–30.

3. In emphasizing both learning and the civic as sites of transformative intersubjectivity, I am taking a cue from Donald W. Harward, cofounder and director of Bringing Theory to Practice. See Harward, "Introduction and Framing Essay," in *Civic Values, Civic Practices,* ed. Donald W. Harward (Washington, DC: Bringing Theory to Practice, 2013), x–xxi.

4. See Susan Sturm, Tim Eatman, John Saltmarsh, and Adam Bush, "Full Participation: Building the Architecture for Diversity and Public Engagement in Higher Education" (white paper, Center for Institutional and Social Change, Columbia University Law School, New York, 2011).

Civic Provocations: Higher Learning, Civic Competency, and Neighborhood Partnerships

iii

Richard Guarasci

THE PROMISE of comprehensive college civic engagement programs lies in their impact on the lives of our college and university students as well as our neighbors, two groups who become intimately connected in powerful ways. Different from direct political participation, which builds democratic structures, civic engagement forges the foundation of a democratic culture by intertwining learning, personal growth, and social relationships around a community of civic practice. For participants, social barriers are reduced, if not eliminated. Friendships are formed. New connections are made. Communities are revived. Campuses are transformed.

As well documented in *A Crucible Moment: College Learning and Democracy's Future* and other key reports,[1] colleges and universities are revisiting their founding missions and goals where school and society are conceived as intimate partners and purposed around educating students for leadership in a democratic society. This retrospective on institutional mission is necessary as we enter an era of economic limits and technological possibilities that are reshaping what and how students learn and faculty teach as well as how colleges deliver, measure, and price learning. This new era is also marked by severe resource constraints for significant parts of society that are challenged by drastic inequities in health care, educational opportunity, and employment. These social realities collide in the neighborhoods that surround many college and university campuses. These fiscal exigencies affecting universities and local neighborhoods became joined to the civic mission of colleges and universities that desperately need to demonstrate their "public good" in order to regain the trust and confidence of the larger society. Challenged neighborhoods need new allies in a period of stagnant support from the federal and state governmental units. A new and symbiotic relationship is required for both universities and neighborhoods to succeed. Although some argue that the very idea of the college campus may soon be obsolete, the connection of student learning to civic purpose holds great promise for the resurrection of place-based learning.

In an age that both promises remarkable technological advances affecting the acquisition of knowledge and portends a reshaping of learning as anonymous and passive, community-based learning holds the key to making place important. While the acquisition of knowledge can be advanced through online resources, the traditional classroom, or a hybrid model using both approaches, it is through civic involvement that students learn how to engage difference, value diversity, encounter and solve problems. In field-based settings, they apply their learning, confront barriers, forge new social relationships built around collaborative practice, and work within community institutions. From these experiences, students come to appreciate their curricular learning as the means through which they gain the expertise, skills, and larger historical, scientific, and humanistic context to make fuller meaning of their community experience. Civic work gives students a greater chance to flourish as it expands their learning beyond that available from a classroom, whether on campus or online.

THE WAGNER PLAN

Like a number of institutions that maintain comprehensive neighborhood partnerships—such as the University of Pennsylvania, Syracuse University, Tulane University, Johns Hopkins University, and Widener University—Wagner College relies on an educational foundation consisting of a comprehensive curricular and cocurricular program that integrates classroom texts, field experience, and civic involvement. Partnership designs vary by institution, but in Wagner's approach (called the Wagner Plan), the principal feature is a commitment to one specific neighborhood on Staten Island, which, with approximately 480,000 residents, is the least populous of New York City's five boroughs. Wagner College's Port Richmond Partnership (hereafter referred to as "the Partnership") focuses on a neighborhood that once was the commercial hub of the borough before the Verrazano Bridge connected it to Brooklyn and the rest of the city in 1964. Then, this neighborhood was predominately made up of various white ethnic groups, mostly of Italian heritage. Fifty years later, it comprises more than 60 percent undocumented Mexican immigrants, 20 percent African Americans, and 20 percent white ethnic New Yorkers. It is a poor community with racial divides, significant disparities in health care, low graduation rates and underresourced schools, high unemployment, and no significant industrial or small-business presence.

THE PORT RICHMOND PARTNERSHIP

In 2007 the experiential component of Wagner's unique curriculum became more focused on civic work, and in 2009 the Partnership was launched to become the centerpiece of this work.

At Wagner College, we conceived of partnerships in a new form that envisions this type of college-civic work as serving as an important anchor in challenged communities. The outcomes of such partnerships are dynamic. They transform learning for students and for neighbors, faculty, and staff—even for a variety of student campus organizations.

The Partnership is organized as a democratic alliance between twenty-plus neighborhood organizations and Wagner College. The Partnership identified four principal policy areas: (1) educational opportunities and college readiness, (2) health care needs and preventative health education, (3) small business economic development, and (4) immigration services and culture and the arts. Each of these policy areas serves as a focal point for directing community-based learning courses, cocurricular civic engagement programs, and voluntary community service activities.

The Partnership is an attempt to integrate the college's civic engagement programs into the identified strategic areas in order to achieve a sustained and effective impact on our neighborhood's challenges. In so doing, the Partnership has succeeded in reducing the incidence of diabetes and obesity, increasing college attendance within the Port Richmond community, advancing sustainable small business development, and increasing literacy and English language proficiency among Port Richmond's Mexican immigrants. And, finally our neighborhood has a flourishing artistic and cultural community.

The college's goals for the Partnership are to increase student learning in specific courses, to increase students' civic competency and intercultural capacity, and to have a discernible impact in the Port Richmond neighborhood across the strategic policy areas. As an example, after working closely with El Centro de Immigrante, one of our partners, a recent Wagner College graduate, characterized the collaborative work as uncovering a "second faculty" within the community from whom she learned much about the real context of these neighborhood challenges. Her liberal arts curriculum provided the cultural, economic, and social foundation needed to grasp these practical problems. This student's major in nursing gave her the tools and practices to be a successful professional in the Port Richmond neighborhood. Ultimately, she found her career calling as a health care professional dedicated to addressing health care disparities.

THE POWER AND CHALLENGES OF NEIGHBORHOOD PARTNERSHIPS

Each type of institutional partnership has varying degrees of impact on student, faculty, and neighborhood cultures. Our assessment data indicate that the overall impact of the Wagner Plan's commitment to experiential learning and civic practice has been impressive, providing positive changes for all participating constituents, from the college to the neighborhood.

The key to successful college-neighborhood partnerships is the establishment of trust and reasonable expectations for both parties. As a result of a comprehensive neighborhood program, the college ethos begins to transform. Students find greater meaning in their courses of study. They discover the true and remarkable assets in the community, such as a rich cultural diversity and different ethnic folkways and values. Through these encounters, students develop self-motivation and agency as they provide needed service to others. Although they may encounter barriers to progress, these experiences prompt development of the skills and discipline required to resolve disputes and solve real-world problems.

CHALLENGES TO SUCCESS

The challenges to realizing this type of transformation are significant. First, the idiosyncratic nature of neighborhood work must be integrated with a curriculum and cocurriculum that has structure, intellectual integrity, and temporal continuity. A traditional service-learning model stands on the academic schedule: courses end and students go home, but neighborhood needs and ongoing programs remain. Consequently, educational experiences must be strung together around curricular and community needs that are aligned with neighborhood projects and organized into strategic policy areas. In a partnership model, administrators, staff, faculty, students, and neighborhood leaders build the relationships, trust, and interactions that produce the community dialogues and assessments necessary to forge a continuous presence and engagement of the college with its neighbors. Together, all participants in the partnership identify the strategic policy area of interest, related projects, and relevant curriculum, thereby drawing the relevant courses to the partnership rather than relying on academically defined courses to search for community partners and placements.

Second, neighborhood partnerships must be sustainable. Given contemporary fiscal realities, these partnership programs must be carefully arranged so that the essential institutional commitment of the college or university is one of social capital. If the academic institution is the source of fiscal outlay, then the longevity of its neighborhood programs is likely to be at risk. Rather, partnership programs require the strategic alignment of teaching and learning assets with neighborhood needs and assets.

Third, student learning is the necessary condition for the success of a partnership. If and only if student learning is enhanced by the partnership may the college's tuition, credit hours, faculty, and staff work be allocated to it. Wagner College judges the success of its Port Richmond Partnership according to three criteria: (1) students' learning from related academic courses must be demonstrated; (2) student civic competency must increase; and (3) discernible community impact in strategic policy or project areas must be measurable over a specific time period.

Fourth, a partnership must be democratic in practice. Community partners, faculty members, civic engagement staff, and administrative leaders must be actively involved in shaping the programs, protocols, and practice of the civic work.

As difficult as these challenges are to satisfy, they hold the key to the transformative power of a liberal education, namely critical thinking and reflective practice. In the end, our goal is for students to graduate as civic professionals.[2]

At Wagner's recent parade of end-of-year academic, athletic, and professional program recognitions, I quietly reflected on how students now frame their college achievements around their civic leadership and service. Whether at a nurse's pinning ceremony, a dinner for academic excellence, a celebration of professional accomplishment, an exhibit of honors theses, a dinner for outstanding student athletes, or a performance by talented student artists—all students name their civic work as the primary contributor to defining themselves and their achievements. They thank faculty, staff, and community partners for their personal growth, their newfound career aspirations, and their life goals. It is remarkable to witness.

NOTES

1. National Task Force on Civic Learning and Democratic Engagement, *A Crucible Moment: College Learning and Democracy's Future* (Washington, DC: Association of American Colleges and Universities, 2012).

2. See William M. Sullivan, *Work and Integrity: The Crisis and Promise of Professionalism in America* (San Francisco: Jossey-Bass, 2005).

Everyone's a Participant: Large-Scale Civic Experiences in the First-Year Curriculum

iv

Thia Wolf

[Learning] combines personal transformation with the evolution of social structures. —ETIENNE WENGER

AT CALIFORNIA STATE UNIVERSITY–CHICO (CSU–Chico), a mid-sized public university in Northern California, all entering students are involved in at least one, and frequently more than one, large-scale civic event. These events, which are embedded in required first-year courses, take the form of either a town hall meeting (embedded in a required American government course) or a great debate (embedded in a required oral communication course). Below, I briefly describe the events and discuss assessment results that document key outcomes for the students and faculty who participate in them. The broader meaning of these events exceeds the confines of our campus, however. By also describing the participation of multiple constituents in these large-scale civic projects, I demonstrate how the events create a meaningful bridge between the campus and the city of Chico.

In 2006, inspired by the insistent call by the president of CSU–Chico for the development of a strong civic dimension in students' education, three faculty members teaching a required first-year writing course designed and helped their students participate in the university's first town hall meeting. In 2009, the event moved from the English department to the political science department. Participation grew rapidly, from a total of 180 participants in the first town hall to totals routinely ranging from 800 to 1,000 participants each semester. The town hall's three-part structure includes an opening plenary with a student keynote speaker; a "breakout" discussion section involving twenty-five students, a facilitator, and expert consultants; and a closing small-group action meeting, called a roundtable, where eight or nine students meet with an expert consultant to form articulated potential action plans based on the students' research on policy issues. The final student assignment is the creation of a written action plan that charts a course through any of the following: additional research; contact plans for connecting with local or national organizations; strategies for forming a new club or organization on campus; well-articulated intentions to contact local, state, and national political representatives; and plans for placing a measure on an upcoming ballot.

Moderators and consultants for the town halls come from both the campus and the surrounding community. Frequent participants include faculty members, campus administrators, directors of nonprofit organizations, city employees, city council members, and educators from local K-12 schools. These individuals volunteer their time, encouraging student voices in both breakout and round-table sessions, moderating student dialogues, and prompting students through questions and problem-posing discussions. Students come prepared to participate in an informed way by completing a required inquiry-research-writing sequence in the American government course. The town hall provides them with a sense of purpose and the motivation to work together toward the shared goal of entering this temporary public sphere.

The great debates, which began in 2009, place oral communication students from the communication arts and sciences department in varied activities focused on contentious issues. Following work on an inquiry-reading-writing sequence, students take their classroom work public. Student, faculty, and community participants engage each other across significant political and personal differences in a civil manner. Participants are reminded throughout the daylong event that the health of a democracy depends on difference, on dialogue, and on a willingness to consider multiple perspectives.

With the City of Chico's consent and support, students take center stage in the city council chambers, the Old Municipal Building, city hall, and an outdoor commons called the Chico City Plaza. Growing rapidly from three hundred to two thousand participants, the great debates have become major city events, bringing together students with varied community members for discussion groups, interactive civic expo exhibits, speeches, presentations, and debates. Political parties set up tables to discuss public issues and upcoming elections with students, and voter registration takes place throughout events, which begin at 9:00 a.m. and conclude at 8:30 p.m.

Assessments of these events show that the students who participate in the town halls are more likely to persist in college. Their four-year profile looks substantially different from that of nonparticipants, with statistically significant positive differences in well-being, civic efficacy, and personal confidence (the belief that "I can make a difference in the world"). Students who participate in the great debates outscore their nonparticipating counterparts on multiple measures, including political interest, community leadership, and academic engagement. Many students participate in both events; in these cases, assessment results show a "double dose" effect, with stronger outcomes in the areas of academic engagement, civic efficacy, and flourishing.

Because the primary focus of these events is on students, it took us a while to notice that this large-scale civic work had also affected the ecology of both the campus and the community. The town halls routinely bring community participants onto the campus, asking them to listen, to share information and experience, and to engage in cross-generation dialogue with the newest adult members of the community. Focus groups with community participants indicate how surprised some are at the students' level of knowledge and commitment regarding public issues ranging from the No Child Left Behind Act to the extended deployment of troops in the Middle East and the mental health issues veterans experience on returning home. Some community members ask to be put on the permanent list of town hall participants; they share their experiences and best practices with newcomers from the community before the events begin.

The great debates rely on community partners, the city manager's office, and the city council to house each eleven-hour event and to take part in the day's activities. The local paper covers the event each semester and now routinely carries a story to remind the community that it will be coming up, as well as providing front-page coverage of the event itself. Community members and, during election times, local political candidates join the students in interactive venues. Recently, a community member wrote a letter to the paper complaining that he could not attend because the event had become too crowded. We responded by moving segments of the great debate to Chico City Plaza, reducing traffic at the site of individual activities, and ensuring better access for everyone who wants to take part.

Significantly, the great debates include consistent participation by members of both the Republican Party and the Tea Party. Initially, conservative members of the local community expressed reluctance to join us at these events, and we experienced painful difficulties around issues of civic trust. Extensive outreach conducted by the faculty coordinator—including personal phone calls, appearances at meetings, and written exchanges—transformed this situation, and politically conservative community members now participate reliably and enthusiastically each semester.

Faculty participants report gaining new insights about teaching and learning through these public-sphere experiences. In focus groups, graduate teaching assistants have highlighted the "relevance" of the civic work embedded in their classes, noting that involvement in the community sparks a different level of interest in learning. "Most students," said one oral communication teaching assistant, "are not enthusiastic about coming to class. Once they took part [in the great debate], they came away with a much better attitude and understanding about what the class is trying to teach." The teaching assistants who participated in the focus groups unanimously valued their participation in civic venues because the civic event work adds a depth and importance to classroom activities.

Most faculty members who engage in public-sphere projects involve themselves in a process of increased collaboration with colleagues, a reconsideration of assignment sequences, and a heightened awareness of their role in preparing students for civic participation. They say they would "not go back" to prior ways of teaching course material, and they spontaneously extend each project's reach by inviting participation from community members and alumni.

This is the story of a campus that is evolving toward stronger, more ubiquitous forms of civic engagement that are delivered through different pathways in the curriculum. The university president's vision and support has helped us do more than we had originally thought we could do, allowing us to construct new opportunities for placing civic engagement at the heart of the institution's daily practices.

Living the Civic:
Brooklyn's Public Scholars

Caitlin Cahill and Michelle Fine

v

WE ENTER THE WORLD OF "CIVIC ENGAGEMENT" through the portal of a community college that enrolls seventeen thousand students, most of whom are immigrants and almost all of whom are working-class. Our work is to build classrooms where the civic talents of students are recognized; where the pedagogies cultivate the cultural wisdom that students import into the academy; where courses are stitched, through public scholarship projects, into community life. We are referring to the Brooklyn Public Scholars project, a City University of New York partnership between the Graduate Center and Kingsborough Community College, designed to build the civic capacity through public scholarship.

President Obama and many others have identified the community college as a site of policy intervention and educational focus, as one of the most exciting educational spaces to engage. In the abstract, we agree. But in the particulars, we are suspect of a national romance that positions community colleges as saviors of the middle class by lifting up working-class students as "productive citizens" who, in a leap and a bound, are supposed to transcend years of disinvestment in public education, high-stakes testing, and structural racism.

Public higher education is increasingly under assault and vulnerable to austerity, bad press, and new audit regimes designed to demonstrate failure and ignore hard-won miracles. Community colleges are bursting at the seams with eager, dedicated students who have often been underprepared in test-factories and yet are hungry to learn and write their signature on the world. As we contend with, witness, and embody the collateral consequences of structural inequity in the neoliberal restructuring of higher education, we consider the critical issues inspired by civic engagement classrooms, research collaborations, and a faculty civic seminar.

Kingsborough Community College is one of the best. Named as one of the top four community colleges in the nation by the Aspen Institute, Kingsborough educates students with an especially wide range of nationalities (140 countries) and languages—Urdu is the second most popular language after English. The students also vary considerably in terms of age, number of children, number of jobs, income, and whether they have official documents or not. Kingsborough students are profoundly dedicated to higher education. Even after struggling in the K-12 system and often confronting failures, they are relentlessly committed to getting it right and pursuing the American Dream. Constantly working to meet and sustain such drive, Kingsborough faculty members each teach nine courses a year.

Kingsborough is a remarkable place in many ways, not least because in 2013 it established a new civic engagement graduation requirement—a vanguard move for a community college. On the campus, this requirement has pried open new conversations about "the civic"—about what it entails and what it looks like in students' lives, in classrooms, and within the culture of the institution. While immigrant students and working-class students typically are portrayed in civic engagement research as though they were "low on engagement," we know this to be untrue. Immigrant and working class students are deeply steeped in their families, neighborhoods, and their home communities, often engaged across national lines. They do not have to venture far in order to "help" someone who is homeless, incarcerated, or facing deportation. They may not donate to causes, but they are sending home remittances. Whether they are caring for family; working and juggling debt; accessing public benefits, public housing, and public education; managing unasked for close relations with law and border enforcement; or advocating for community change, Kingsborough students are 'civic,' they live civic, and they embody collective responsibility. More than simply honoring students whose hard-lived lives are already always public, our work values their unique vantage point on structural inequities and takes seriously their everyday struggles as sites worthy of civic inquiry.

The challenge for our project is not so much to encourage civic engagement among students, but rather to cultivate a campus culture in which the civic expertise that our students bring is appreciated and extended as academic knowledge, research, and the "civic." With this in mind, we scaffold classrooms where students can engage in rigorous public scholarship in order to make sense of the dynamics that they live and to build explicit knowledge between everyday experience and the theoretical concepts they grapple with in class. We generate new knowledge and practices by working with community-based organizations, both on and off campus, in order to interrogate questions of justice and injustice in schools and communities—questions related to environmentalism, food justice, health care, and class politics.

Exercising their "right to research,"[1] students are raising critical questions about the communities where they live, work, play, and go to school. Students in the Brooklyn Public Scholars classes say they feel more motivated to learn when they can raise questions pertaining to their lives, and others' lives, and when their histories, struggles, and communities sit, alongside those of others, at the center of an engaged curriculum. Critical civic research is not only an essential capacity for democratic citizenship; it is also connected to the capacity to aspire, plan, hope, desire, and achieve one's goals. This cannot be overstated for community college students who have endured the cumulative effects of material injustices and assaults on dignity due to educational disinvestment.

While the impact of participating in public scholarship courses is palpable for the students, we are also inspired by how civic praxis has informed new ways for faculty to create community in their classrooms, through their research, with each other, and beyond the borders of the campus. At the heart of the Brooklyn Public Scholarship project is the Faculty Civic Seminar, a "homespace," as bell hooks would say,[2] a sort of refuge where faculty working hard, long, and uphill can come together to think intellectually and ethically about pedagogy of/for/with the civic. The Faculty Civic Seminar has fostered a space for interdisciplinary thinking for up to twenty faculty members to engage with the theory and practice of public scholarship and develop new civically-engaged courses. Culinary faculty teach an urban cooking class and sit beside biologists whose students are tracking horse-shoe crabs on the beaches of Brooklyn. These biologists, in turn, sit beside a lawyer and urban studies professor who is working with students on a transit justice project and another faculty member who is teaching English to international students through a curriculum designed to address their concerns about going to college. We have faculty who are implementing a multicultural counseling curriculum, one that is sensitive to dynamics of power and through which students teach each other about issues faced by their communities and those they plan to serve. And these faculty share stories with other faculty whose students are involved in a neighborhood "guerilla mapping" project to signify the great women who have kept working-class communities safe and loving.

In some ways, the faculty seminar functions as a kind of sanctuary, holding the neoliberal forces at bay that impinge upon community colleges across the country: the pressure to be aligned with narrow metrics, PowerPoint-ification, dominance of textbooks and testing, and online-ification of community college curriculum. But this is too simple and romantic a vision. Like faculty members at community colleges across the country, dedicated and besieged, the Kingsborough faculty must contend with structural disinvestment and neoliberal "accountability" regimes on an everyday basis. Institutional support for the Brooklyn Public Scholars project has been strong even as we struggle over how to ensure that the institution credits educators' deep commitments, how to assure both release time and a supportive institutional review board process for public scholarship, and how to reconcile deep civic work with the need to build the capacities of students who come out of public high schools that have long been sacrificed to test-prep regimes.

For community college faculty who are running from class to class with barely a moment to catch their breath, the Brooklyn Public Scholars Faculty Civic Seminar provides a time and space to pause, slow down, break bread with each other, and engage collectively and intellectually. Faculty members discuss their students and their own "aha" moments, their research findings, the institutional battles over civic engagement, and the ongoing efforts to gain institutional recognition for their pathbreaking work. In the seminar, faculty are first and foremost scholars. Engaging in collective critical inquiry on the meaning of "the civic" and "the public" in their students' lives can feel like a welcome move to those who have had little time to indulge their own research in a participatory intellectual space. One faculty member described the Brooklyn Public Scholars project as a place where "I feel like I'm part of something larger than my own classroom or project." She wasn't sure what to call this—a community? "Yes, maybe. But that's not quite it." Instead, she said, "maybe it's just about being part of a collective conversation that's about the big picture, about the politics and theory that surround what we're doing."

MOVING TO "SCALE" AT A COMMUNITY COLLEGE THROUGH HORIZONTAL RELATIONS OF DEMOCRACY, EQUITY, INQUIRY, AND ACTION

The Brooklyn Public Scholars project has tried to engage and cultivate the civic through five "connective tissue" areas of a sprawling urban campus. First, the *policy environment* for civic engagement is in place: Kingsborough has a civic engagement requirement, which of course we want to keep thoughtful, reflective, meaningful, and not technical. The terms of the civic engagement mandate are being struggled over, and the Brooklyn Public Scholars faculty are well positioned to contribute to this institutional debate. Second, there is the question of the *institutional infrastructure,* which, at an underfunded college, is always precarious and in process. Third, there are our *classrooms,* sites of desire and struggle where we come to respect students who dare to return to a site where they have found meaning. For many, the classroom is a site of failure and challenge, but also one to which they return in order to engage projects that address questions of justice in their communities.

Fourth, we have strengthened and rendered porous the *membrane of responsibility and reciprocity* between our college and our communities. Raising critical questions as to what counts as a legitimate civic space that is worthy of inquiry, we want to pry open the civic engagement discourse and take a wider view of the landscape of students' everyday lives and communities. Centering the urgent concerns and struggles of students' families and neighborhoods is vital to a renewed politics of civic and community engagement. Whether documenting the life experiences of other immigrant students, researching health hazards of a local waste transfer station, or identifying the necessary academic supports for first-generation community college students, "community" is close to home— and sometimes, it *is* home. Our project also challenges the false distinction between college and community by reframing the college campus itself as the community, as both a unit of analysis and a site of intervention. Perhaps surprisingly, for community college students the campus itself is one of the most meaningful communities to engage. They delve into their own educational concerns through community-based research and action focused on addressing issues related to clean bathrooms, healthy cafeteria food, support for ESL students, and peer mentoring. Last but not least, we have our Faculty Civic Seminar. This *critical intellectual space* is a supportive collective space of participatory leadership where faculty eat, drink wine, kvetch, and engage in deep discussions about pedagogy, research, and the everyday politics of institutional change. And faculty write together! There is now interest in publishing a book of essays by our faculty to explore the intellectual, ethical, and cultural spaces that public scholarship can nurture.

If community colleges are to continue to push beyond technical and vocational focuses and remain intellectually and ethically relevant to students and their communities, then, within the context of the community college itself, we must explore the potential role of critical inquiry and engaged scholarship in strengthening and sustaining the social compact. Our work with the Brooklyn Public Scholarship project is grounded in a commitment to the civic through an interrogation of the student and faculty gifts that too often go unrecognized in institutions that are sedimented into profound structural inequities. Together, we can build classrooms and spaces for faculty engagement as a platform for collective action in order to scaffold the academic and emotional well-being of students and faculty, to support the struggles of our precious and burdened communities, and to honor the public institutions that sustain us all.

ACKNOWLEDGMENTS
We are most grateful to the Brooklyn Public Scholars Faculty for their inspired engagement, critical insights, and commitment to public scholarship. Special thanks to Michelle Billies, Jason VanOra, Peter Fiume, and Jason Leggett for their thoughtful comments on this essay. Much gratitude to María Elena Torre, Nancy Barnes, Gregory Donovan, and Sonia Sanchez for their work on this project.

NOTES
1. See Arjun Appaduri, "The Right to Research," *Globalisation, Societies and Education* 4, no. 2 (2006): 167–77.
2. See bell hooks, *Yearning: Race, Gender, and Cultural Politics* (Boston: South End Press, 1999), 145–53.

Integrating Global and Local Civic Learning (Early and Often)

Nigel Boyle

TWO REFORM MOVEMENTS are currently at work within US higher education—one centered on restoring the civic mission of colleges and universities, and another advocating for global education and the comprehensive internationalization of institutions. The perspective offered here is that restoring the civic and embracing the global are neither discrete nor merely complementary educational objectives. Their *combination* opens up exciting opportunities for transformative learning, and this combination is best effected *early* in the undergraduate experience. Early combination addresses three major pedagogical challenges to achieving these objectives: the "episodic" tyranny of the semester-long course or program; the need to be inclusive of all students; and the neglect of the non-cognitive, psychosocial aspect of student development.

Proliferating civic engagement centers at US colleges and universities are underpinned by a range of ethical/political missions that runs along a spectrum of benevolence, from service to social justice. The more ambitious centers identify the goal of ensuring that students understand the structural causes of the conditions they encounter experientially through projects, the need for reciprocity in college-community partnerships, and the importance of the academy working on community-defined priorities. Pedagogical goals vary considerably, with the more ambitious addressing Martha Nussbaum's trifecta: critical thinking and self-examination; the capacity to see one's fate as connected to that of others; and the ability to empathize, to imagine oneself in another's place.[1]

Ongoing, long-term partnerships with community-based or civic organizations address one of the traditional shortcomings of service projects, namely, the episodic nature of quarter- or semester-long time frames. The ability to cycle students (and faculty) through an ongoing project does much to benefit community organizations and avoid burning out activist faculty. But two significant problems remain: (1) giving students ample opportunities to reflect on community or civic engagement and the (measurable) cognitive and non-cognitive development they undergo, and (2) involving *all* students and faculty in such engaged learning, rather than just the "usual suspects"—civic engagement for the physicists as well as the sociologists.

The ethical and political challenges posed by local civic engagement exist in magnified form in global civic engagement and study abroad. Ivan Illich's famous 1968 screed, "To Hell with Good Intentions," pilloried US international student volunteerism as useless "mission vacations," at best, and malignant proselytizing, at worst.[2] Study abroad programming runs the gamut from glorified tourism to programming that promotes active engagement with local cultures and communities. The most common forms follow either the "exchange" model, according to which students take classes and live in dorms in circumstances not unlike those at their home campus, or the cultural immersion model, according to which students "homestay," live in, study in, and become participants in communities abroad. The latter model yields opportunities for community-engaged research. But all study abroad programs run the risk that the experience will be, in essence, a student "sabbatical"—a delightful, in-and-out, hermetically sealed episode disconnected from the rest of college education. As with local civic engagement, study abroad programming struggles to give students the time to reflect on and process the cognitive and non-cognitive aspects of their experience. It also struggles to be inclusive of all students and faculty—global engagement for the math majors as well as French literature majors.

Students who go abroad typically do so during their junior year. Students who become deeply civically engaged typically do so in the latter part of their undergraduate careers. Experience with both of these exoteric practices comes late, after the major has been declared and after the early part of students' careers has been focused on the esoteric culture of the college campus. This is doubly unfortunate, as it means that the engagement experiences cannot shape the rest of a student's academic program, including the planning of the major—engagement practices are add-ons, rather than formative events. Moreover, "belated" global and local engagement practices don't allow sufficient time and space for reflective understanding of these experiences, especially their non-cognitive aspects. It would be better for students to become engaged in local civic engagement and study abroad early in their academic careers, before they are "branded" by their disciplines. These practices should be a part of general education, rather than boutique experiences for a select few in certain disciplines.

Civic engagement and study abroad are exoteric "high-impact practices" that involve experiential, face-to-face interaction with people outside the college community. This is especially true of the deeper varieties of each, cultural immersion study abroad programs and social justice–oriented civic engagement programs—practices that "disrupt the established ecology of atomized courses, disciplinary courses of study, and the separation of curricular from cocurricular experiences."[3] For institutions committed to both civic engagement and global education, the ability to connect programming in the two fields opens up possibilities for sequential and dialectical programming.

The Institute for Global-Local Action and Study at Pitzer College is charged with proactively building linkages between civic engagement and global education, utilizing the infrastructure provided by the college's local community partnerships and cultural immersion programs in communities abroad. In 2013, with support from Bringing Theory to Practice, Pitzer launched a pilot program designed to explore how global and local civic learning practices can be further cultivated in order to address the three pedagogical challenges noted above: practices being isolated episodes, failing to be inclusive of all students, and failing to address the psychosocial well-being of students. The program reflects a "Jesuitical" strategy of getting students civically engaged as *early* as possible in their academic careers. Focused on the 2013–14 freshman class, the project entails a two-year intensive mentorship program involving faculty advisors and residential life staff. During this mentorship period, students are "fast tracked" into early—and repeated—participation in civic engagement courses and projects; early—and repeated—participation in immersive study abroad programming focused on civic engagement, starting in the sophomore year; and early declaration of majors, with a focus on integrating local and global engagement activity into majors across all fields. Each student develops a two-year plan for global-local engagement that, during the freshman year, includes participation on an "action research team" and an alternative spring break study tour to a Pitzer program abroad. During the sophomore year, the students take other courses that meet the college's social responsibility requirement, and they are required to spend one semester abroad on a cultural immersion program.

"Fast-tracking" students into local civic engagement and study abroad creates the possibility for iterated and dialectical experiences, with ample opportunity to reflect, regret, reconsider, and retry. For example, a freshman year internship at a local youth detention camp can be followed by a sophomore experience in the criminal justice system in Ecuador. Subsequent engagement experiences in the junior and senior years allow for cumulative intellectual and visceral student development. The pilot project is intended to connect over time what might otherwise be isolated "episodes" in a student's career, and it is inclusive of all students, not just a self-selected subset.

Combining the restoration of the civic mission of colleges with global education can lead to transformative global and local learning. If global and local initiatives can be infused early in student's college career, then such learning can become central to the formative intellectual and personal experience of all students, rather than the marginal experience of a few.

NOTES

1. Martha Nussbaum, *Cultivating Humanity: A Classical Defense of Reform in Liberal Education* (Cambridge, MA: Harvard University Press, 1997).
2. Ivan Illich, "To Hell with Good Intentions" (address to the Conference on InterAmerican Student Projects, Cuernavaca, Mexico, April 20, 1968).
3. David Scobey, "Why Now? Because This Is a Copernican Moment," in *Civic Provocations,* ed. Donald W. Harward (Washington, DC: Bringing Theory to Practice, 2012), 4.

Civic-Minded Professors

Barry Checkoway

SHOULD A COLLEGE OR UNIVERSITY have a strategy for strengthening the civic-mindedness of its professors? And if so, what should it be?

Civic-mindedness is a way of thinking about, and paying attention to, the public good and the well-being of society. It can take many forms, such as when people show passion for a social issue by organizing an action group or planning a local program. It can also be expressed by teaching a course or by working on a research project and presenting the findings to municipal officials in addition to professional peers. There is no single form of civic-mindedness; as long as people are thinking in terms of the public good, they are being civic-minded.

Faculty members are ideally positioned for civic-mindedness. They develop knowledge that can contribute to the civic, teach courses that prepare students for public roles, and share information and ideas outside the academy. They are based in well-resourced anchor institutions whose influence extends from neighborhood to nation. As the following examples demonstrate, almost any faculty member can integrate the civic into their normal professional work:

- A physics professor lectures on velocity and relates this to automobile accidents. He explores theories through a mock accident, examines impacts at varying speeds, and prepares students for presentations to safety officials. As a final assignment, students must write papers on "physics for change"— an assignment that has parallels in biology, chemistry, and other sciences.
- An English professor teaches composition as "writing in the public sphere." Students organize around policy problems, engage in class discussions, and make presentations at town hall meetings. The students strengthen their writing skills and their civic competencies through "public work" that contributes to learning in other arts and humanities fields.
- A mathematics professor has expertise in ethnomathematics and studies the mathematics of Native Americans. He teaches a calculus course that draws on cultural traditions, chairs a task force on minorities in mathematics, and receives an award from the college. His integration of research and teaching with his civic commitments inspires his colleagues in algebra, geometry, and game theory.
- A psychology professor studies the effects of intergroup dialogue on students of diverse social identities. She engages students in courses that affect their understanding of themselves and their commitment to civic action. She

appears in the media and makes the case for diversity to the state board of education, a source of great pride to the institution.

Civic-minded faculty members can be found in academic disciplines and professional fields—such as art, business, classics, engineering, medicine, and zoology—and among the faculty who serve as department chairs, deans, vice presidents, provosts, and presidents. They are often among the highly productive people on campus, in the scope of their research and student evaluations of their teaching. They are not necessarily typical of the professoriate, but they are there, and are highly effective in their roles.

Despite the productivity of these professors, however, there also are obstacles to civic-mindedness. First, most faculty members are trained in graduate schools whose curricula ignore civic content, and they are conditioned to believe that civic-mindedness is not central to their work.

Second, faculty members are not necessarily rewarded by the institution. The present reward structures of most colleges and universities—including promotion and tenure processes—are usually silent on civic-mindedness. Faculty members are asked about their number of publications in peer-reviewed journals, but not about how these relate to the public good and welfare of society.

In the academy, however, work that draws upon faculty members' disciplinary expertise is rightly recognized as legitimate. And when faculty members organize their research and teaching in ways that allow them to draw upon that expertise while also keeping the public good in mind, they should be rewarded, although this is not normal at the present time.

If faculty members were asked to report on an annual basis about the civic effects of their research and teaching, and this were to become an expectation for performance evaluation, then the outcomes would be extraordinary, for both the individual and the institution. Numerous colleges and universities have formulated ways to evaluate work of this type—for example, Michigan State, Minnesota, North Carolina, Pennsylvania, and Portland State—and there is a wealth of information about policies, best practices, and exemplary portfolios at Campus Compact, Community Campus Partnerships for Health, and other national networks and sources.[1]

When Thomas Kuhn introduced the term "paradigm shift," he had science in mind. He argued that science undergoes periodic revolutions in which the nature of inquiry is transformed—not by research, but rather by scholars who experience a change in their thinking and who, as a result, view the world in a different way. Kuhn used the example of the transition from a Ptolemaic cosmology to a Copernican one—from a cosmology with Earth at the center of the universe to one with the Sun at the center. When he wrote about the Copernican revolution, some scholars embraced his ideas and agreed that paradigm shifts do happen.[2]

But even the most civic-minded of professors do not spend their days dealing with cosmological changes in the universe. Rather, they write research papers, teach courses, meet students, and attend faculty meetings. With all due respect to these revolutionary ideas, professors are preparing for class.

Should a college or university have a strategy for enabling faculty members to become more civic-minded in their professional work? Yes, but what would it be? Faculty members are well positioned for civic-mindedness, and many are quietly yearning to relate their work to the well-being of society. Indeed, there is nothing a priori to prevent professors in any discipline from making their research and teaching more civic in their content and process. If professors choose not to view themselves or their work in civic terms, this is not to suggest that they might not do so if it were expected of them.

What would it take? Some of my colleagues have ideas about changes that they believe might make the institution more civic. Change doctoral programs and graduate education. Change the reward structure. Change the institution. Change the president and provost. I love these ideas. But if I were to devote myself to them, I probably would want to become the president or provost. At the present time, however, I am a faculty member and engaged scholar who believes that, in addition to needed changes at the college or university level, the power of the institution resides with the faculty. Without the faculty, nothing lasting is likely to happen.

I can imagine an institution whose faculty members are reaching out to their colleagues and making the case for the civic as integral to their professional self-interest, and who are helping their colleagues think about how their work contributes to the public good. I can imagine these faculty members forming a small group whose members themselves reach out to other colleagues and involve them in the conversation. Such a group might organize a workshop on how to integrate civic-mindedness into research and teaching, and then convene a faculty conference in order to hear from allies such as presidents who have platforms on which to campaign, provosts who manage institutional procedures, faculty leaders who are civic-minded already, and students who have more power than they realize.

Should a college or university have a strategy for strengthening the civic mindedness of its professors? Yes. But just because I can imagine it does not make it so. Yet, it might well be that the most basic institutional changes are ones that are within reach of each and every faculty member, many of whom can incorporate the civic into his or her research and teaching tomorrow. After all, there was worldwide resistance to the Copernican idea before it spread. Kuhn would surely say that paradigm shifts are built partly on increasing awareness among college and university faculty members and that with ongoing organizing, resistance to civic-mindedness would be minuscule in comparison to the cosmological revolution he described.

NOTES

1. See Julie Ellison and Timothy K. Eatman, *Scholarship in Public: Knowledge Creation and Tenure Policy in the Engaged University* (Syracuse, NY: Imagining America, 2008), http://imaginingamerica.org/wp-content/uploads/2011/05/TTI_FINAL.pdf; Catherine Jordan, Sarena Seifer, Lorilee Sandmann, and Sherril Gelmon, "Development of a Mechanism for the Peer Review and Dissemination of Innovative Products of Community-Engaged Scholarship," *International Journal of Prevention Practice and Research* 1, no. 1 (2009): 21–8; Tami L. Moore and Kelly K. Ward, "Documenting Engagement: Faculty Perspectives on Self-Representation for Promotion and Tenure," *Journal of Higher Education Outreach and Engagement* 12, no. 4, (2008) 5–24; Hiram E. Fitzgerald, Cathy Burack, and Sarena Seifer, *Handbook of Engaged Scholarship: Institutional Change* (Lansing, MI: Michigan State University Press, 2010).

2. Thomas S. Kuhn, *The Structure of Scientific Revolutions*, 3rd ed. (Chicago: University of Chicago Press, 1996).

Contributors

Nigel Boyle is associate dean for global and local programs, director of the Institute for Global/Local Action & Study (IGLAS), and IGLAS Chair in Political Studies at Pitzer College.

Nancy Cantor is chancellor of Rutgers University-Newark; from 2004 to 2013, she served as chancellor of Syracuse University.

Caitlin Cahill is assistant professor of Urban Geography & Politics at Pratt Institute.

Barry Checkoway is professor of social work and of urban and regional planning at the University of Michigan.

Peter Englot is senior vice chancellor for public affairs and chief of staff at Rutgers University-Newark; from 2006 to 2013, he served as associate vice president for public affairs at Syracuse University.

Michelle Fine is Distinguished Professor of Psychology at the City University of New York Graduate Center.

Richard Guarasci is president of Wagner College.

Peter Hajnal is founding co-dean for curriculum at Bard College Berlin.

Robert M. Hollister is professor of urban and environmental policy and planning at Tufts University and executive director of the Talloires Network, a global coalition of universities that are moving beyond the ivory tower.

Paul LeBlanc is president of Southern New Hampshire University.

Richard K. Miller is president of the Franklin W. Olin College of Engineering.

Brian Murphy is president of De Anza College.

Thomas Nørgaard is founding co-dean for curriculum at Bard College Berlin.

Thomas L. "Les" Purce is president of the Evergreen State College.

Darby K. Ray is director of the Harward Center for Community Partnerships and the Donald W. and Ann M. Harward Professor of Civic Engagement at Bates College.

Jill N. Reich is professor of psychology at Bates College and senior scholar of the Bringing Theory to Practice project. From 1999 to 2011, she served as academic vice president and dean of faculty at Bates College.

Thia Wolf is director of the First-Year Experience Program and professor of English at California State University–Chico.

Bringing Theory to Practice (BTtoP) is an independent project in partnership with the Association of American Colleges and Universities. It is supported by the S. Engelhard Center (whose major contributors include the Charles Engelhard Foundation and the Christian A. Johnson Endeavor Foundation, in addition to other foundations and individuals).

BTtoP encourages colleges and universities to assert their core purposes as educational institutions not only to advance learning and discovery, but also to advance both the potential and well-being of each student as a whole person and education as a public good that sustains a civic society.

BTtoP supports campus-based initiatives that demonstrate how uses of engaged forms of learning that actively involve students, both within and beyond the classroom, can contribute directly to their cognitive, emotional, and civic development. The work of the project is conducted primarily through sponsored research, conferences, grants to colleges and universities of all types, and publications—notably including *Transforming Undergraduate Education: Theory that Compels and Practices that Succeed,* edited by Donald W. Harward (Lanham, MD: Rowman & Littlefield, 2012.).

BTtoP provides a rare source of intellectual and practical assistance to all institutional constituencies that are seeking to make or strengthen the changes needed to realize their missions of learning and discovery, and that are working to create campus cultures for learning that recognize the necessary connections among higher learning, students well-being, and civic engagement.

Information about current grant opportunities, project publications, and forthcoming conferences is available online at **www.BTtoP.org**.